Waiting on the Word

Waiting on the Word

A Poem a day for Advent,
Christmas and Epiphany

Malcolm Guite

CANTERBURY
PRESS

Norwich

© Malcolm Guite 2015

First published in 2015 by the Canterbury Press Norwich
Editorial office
3rd Floor, Invicta House,
108–114 Golden Lane,
London EC1Y 0TG, UK

Canterbury Press is an imprint of Hymns Ancient & Modern Ltd
(a registered charity)
13A Hellesdon Park Road, Norwich,
Norfolk NR6 5DR, UK

www.canterburypress.co.uk

Scripture quotations are from the New Revised Standard Version of
the Bible, Anglicized Edition, copyright © 1989, 1995 by the Division
of Christian Education of the National Council of the Churches of
Christ in the USA. Used by permission. All rights reserved.

British Library Cataloguing in Publication data

A catalogue record for this book is available
from the British Library

978 1 84825 800 6

Typeset by Regent Typesetting
Printed and bound in Great Britain by
CPI Group (UK) Ltd, Croydon

Contents

Acknowledgements

I am very grateful to the contemporary poets David Baird, Richard Bauckham, Scott Cairns, David Grieve, Grevel Lindop and Luci Shaw for their personal permission to print some of their poems in this anthology.

I would also like to express particular thanks to Travis Helms for his invaluable help as an amanuensis, his presence as a conversation partner, and his many insights and suggestions, which have helped so much in the making of this book.

Introduction

Advent is a paradoxical season: a season of waiting and antici-
pation in which the waiting itself is strangely rich and fulfilling,
a season that looks back at the people who waited in darkness
for the coming light of Christ and yet forward to a fuller light
still to come and illuminate our darkness. Advent falls in winter,
at the end of the year, in the dark and cold, but its focus is on
the coming of light and life, when the Ancient of Days becomes
a young child and says, 'Behold, I make all things new.' Perhaps
only poetry can help us fathom the depths and inhabit the ten-
sions of these paradoxes.

The Latin root of the familiar word 'Advent' is *veni*. It speaks
of 'coming', the coming of Christ in every way. And in that sense
the advent of Christ has for us a triple focus, not simply the classic
double focus of the Prayer Book's beautiful and familiar Advent
Collect. That collect speaks of Christ's first coming 'to visit us in
great humility' in the manger of Bethlehem, then leaps across time
to the fulfilment and finality of all things: Christ's second com-
ing 'in his glorious majesty'. Of course, we need these two great
advents to frame the in-between time in which we live; they are
the alpha and the omega, as it were, in the lexicon of our lives. But
surely, between this beginning and this end there are many other
advents. 'Lo, I am with you always, even unto the end of the age,'
says Jesus. 'Whatsoever you do unto the least of these, you do it
unto me'; 'This is my body, this is my blood.' In our encounters
with the poor and the stranger, in the mystery of the sacraments,
in those unexpected moments of transfiguration surely there is
also an advent and Christ comes to us. Perhaps that is why the
other sense we have of the word 'advent' is to find it beginning the

word 'adventure'. The knights in Sir Thomas Malory's *Le Morte d'Arthur* say to one another, 'Let us take the adventure that God sends us,' recognizing that the God in whom we live and move and have our being may come and meet us when and where he pleases, and any door we open may be the door to the 'chapel perilous'.

In selecting a poem to read for each day in Advent I have been mindful of these three kinds of coming, and mindful too of those paradoxes of past and future, dark and light, waiting and consolation, emptiness and fulfilment. I hope that readers of this anthology will have a sense of both the familiar and of adventuring upon the new. I have drawn upon some spiritual classics (though not all of these will be familiar to every modern reader), from Edmund Spenser, John Donne and George Herbert forward through great nineteenth-century poets and hymnodists like Christina Rossetti. But also included are poets who may be new to most readers: unjustly neglected poets of the twentieth century, particularly Ruth Pitter and Anne Ridler, and a sampling from some contemporary Christian poets who are continuing and reimagining the spiritual tradition in which Herbert and Rossetti were working, such as Scott Cairns and Luci Shaw.

This anthology moves through Advent into its fulfilment in Christmas, and indeed on to the day of Epiphany. The coming of the magi in Epiphany has also guided me more broadly in my choice of poetry. Pagan wise men following the star of their own best and highest learning were brought even by that to the stable, though of course at the stable there was something new to learn. So I have included in the Advent part of this anthology poetry by non-Christian poets who seem, nevertheless, to see in the heavens such signs as declare the glory of the Lord. One virtue of keeping the seasons of the sacral year is that they can help us to redress an imbalance, either in our own spiritual life or in the culture of our church or denomination. Advent, with its special and natural emphasis on Mary the mother of our Lord, carrying the child, in the deepest possible ways preparing intimately for his advent into the world and into her life, can be especially helpful for Protestants, whose culture has for purely historical reasons tended to eclipse her, and a number of the poems dwell on Mary's joyful and sorrowful mysteries.

This question of redressing an imbalance leads me to mention a final aim for this anthology, which is to help us restore that quietness, that inner peace, that willingness to wait unfulfilled in the dark, in the midst of a season that conspires to do nothing but fling bling and tinsel at us right through December. I hope that readers will feel that they are joining me in what is a profoundly countercultural and indeed subversive act (and one thing that would make it even more countercultural would be to dare to read these poems aloud and slowly, in defiance of the silent skim-reading that has replaced an older tasting of language). Reclaiming Advent's rich fast will restore meaning to the even richer feast when Christmas comes.

Finally, a comment about the theology that is embodied and explored in this book and its companion volume *The Word in the Wilderness*. Although these two books are anthologies – gatherings of poetry and responses to poetry, open and devotional in character, appealing to the imagination – and not formal works of theology or pieces of academic discourse, they are intended to be a contribution to that great enquiry through which faith seeks understanding. For that is how St Anselm helpfully defined theology.

In my book *Faith, Hope and Poetry: Theology and the Poetic Imagination*, I made the case for the imagination as a truth-bearing faculty. I suggested that we must avail ourselves of the imagination in a way that complements our use of reason, if we are to come close to understanding the apprehensions of our faith. In these two books I have tried to put that theory into practice. I believe that by 'waiting on the Word', in every sense of that phrase, waiting on the true Logos, the meaning behind all meanings, and attending closely to the way that meaning is imaginatively bodied forth in poetry, we can begin to unfold a little more of the mystery of our faith, to unpack and open out the contents of those technical words, Incarnation and Atonement. It is my conviction that to do theology well we must bring the poets to the table along with the theologians, and listen carefully to what they say. I hope that

these two books will be a small contribution to that long, aston-
ished and unfinished conversation which is Christian theology.

A Note on How to Use This Book

A word about the ordering of poems in this book. To start us off, and set some of our themes, is Christina Rossetti's comparatively little known poem 'Advent Sunday'. That day may, of course, fall at the end of November or the beginning of December, but this poem can be read in addition to the one for the day assigned. Thereafter, one poem a day is given from 1 December through to the Feast of Epiphany on 6 January. Some days have their fixed and particular meanings, as with Christmas Eve and Christmas Day itself, and to these I have added the days traditionally set for the recital of the seven great 'O Antiphons', from 17 to 23 December. To these Advent Antiphons I have added the sonnet sequence I wrote in response to them. But apart from these set days, the reader may prefer to dip into the anthology without respect to date, or perhaps to gather and cluster poems from different days that explore similar themes.

ADVENT SUNDAY

Advent Sunday *Christina Rossetti*

Behold, the Bridegroom cometh: go ye out
With lighted lamps and garlands round about
To meet Him in a rapture with a shout.

It may be at the midnight, black as pitch,
Earth shall cast up her poor, cast up her rich.

It may be at the crowing of the cock
Earth shall upheave her depth, uproot her rock.

For lo, the Bridegroom fetcheth home the Bride:
His Hands are Hands she knows, she knows His Side.

Like pure Rebekah at the appointed place,
Veiled, she unveils her face to meet His Face.

Like great Queen Esther in her triumphing,
She triumphs in the Presence of her King.

His Eyes are as a Dove's, and she's Dove-eyed;
He knows His lovely mirror, sister, Bride.

He speaks with Dove-voice of exceeding love,
And she with love-voice of an answering Dove.

Behold, the Bridegroom cometh: go we out
With lamps ablaze and garlands round about
To meet Him in a rapture with a shout.

This extraordinary poem of Christina Rossetti's deserves to be better known. At first blush it seems that she has taken only the second and final coming of the Advent Collect, which is one of the many subtle subtexts of this poem. But as we read the poem through, we find not just the familiar and always lurid apocalyptic imagery of the last day and a general resurrection, with the earth casting up both poor and rich; rather we find, gathered from Christ's parables and from Rossetti's intimate and extensive acquaintance with scripture, a series of personal encounters, face to face. Indeed, the scriptural phrase, 'face to face', with its almost chiasmic symmetry, might stand as an emblem for the way in which this poem, which itself uses the image of a mirror, presents us with mutually reflective, beholding, encountering pairs. Again and again a word or phrase is offered up and then returned, transformed, as though the poem were a mimesis of coming and coming again. So within each line we find echoes and answerings ('Bridegroom ... Bride', 'Hands are Hands', 'she knows, she knows', 'Veiled ... unveils', 'her face ... His Face', 'Eyes ... as a Dove's ... Dove-eyed', 'Dove-voice of exceeding love ... love-voice of an answering Dove'), and all these little mirrorings are framed by the great antiphonal mirroring of the two three-line stanzas that open and close the poem, with 'a rapture and a shout'.

Let's look in detail at some of the images she has given us. She frames the poem in the context both of the Collect for Advent Sunday and of Christ's story of the maidens with their lighted lamps awaiting the coming of the bridegroom (Matthew 25.1–13). Rossetti takes the Gospel phrases and opens them out profoundly. 'It may be at the midnight' leads to that sharp observation that the poor and the rich must rise to the same judgement, but surely the careful rhyming of 'rich' with 'pitch' carries its own warning. Likewise, to mark the dawn with the phrase 'the crowing of the cock' summons echoes of Christ's words to Peter about betrayal before the cock crows; but with them, answering echoes of how that betrayal might be restored by renewed love. Then comes a sequence of couplets in which Rossetti is perhaps offering to a patriarchal Victorian culture insights that could only come from a feminine perspective: 'His Hands are Hands she knows, she knows His Side'. Here the Church becomes truly herself, not in powerful triumph, but when she acknowledges the wounds she shares with Christ:

> Like pure Rebekah at the appointed place,
> Veiled, she unveils her face to meet His Face.

There is something strikingly active in the verb 'unveils' here. It is the bride herself and no other figure that does the unveiling. Rebekah is taking charge of the event! And this leads us to an even stronger image of a key woman in scripture: 'Queen Esther in her triumphing'. She triumphs in the presence of her king. Here Rossetti seems to be suggesting that acknowledging the kingship of Christ, far from being a demeaning, belittling or infantilizing act on behalf of the submissive Church, is in fact a radiant affirmation of her own royalty.

1 DECEMBER

The Glance *George Herbert*

   When first thy sweet and gracious eye
Vouchsaf'd ev'n in the midst of youth and night
To look upon me, who before did lie
        Weltring in sinne;
   I felt a sugred strange delight,
Passing all cordials made by any art,
Bedew, embalme, and overrunne my heart,
        And take it in.

   Since that time many a bitter storm
My soul hath felt, ev'n able to destroy,
Had the malicious and ill-meaning harm
        His swing and sway:
   But still thy sweet originall joy
Sprung from thine eye, did work within my soul,
And surging griefs, when they grew bold, controll,
        And got the day.

   If thy first glance so powerfull be,
A mirth but open'd and seal'd up again;
What wonders shall we feel, when we shall see
        Thy full-ey'd love!
   When thou shalt look us out of pain,
And one aspect of thine spend in delight
More then a thousand sunnes disburse in light,
        In heav'n above.

What might this moving and mysterious little poem have to offer us as we come to dark December and begin our Advent journey together? We reflected in the Introduction on how Advent has a triple focus framed by the advent of Christ: the first advent, the revelation of who Christ is at Christmas at the beginning, and the promise of a full, great, final advent at the end of all things; but constantly opening our eyes to the other in-between advents, in which we get glimpses of how the Lord who has come in the beginning and will come in the end still comes to us now. Certainly Herbert's poem reflects something of this frame. It looks back to a beginning with the words 'When first', and concludes with a second framing temporal reference, 'When thou shalt', meditating on how both the memory of the first glance and the anticipation at last of 'full-ey'd love' can sustain us even in dark December's in-between time.

But first we must consider the title and what might be meant spiritually by 'The Glance'. The glance of the deity – to be suddenly caught in the gaze of the divine, to be invited beyond all hope, and in fear and trembling – is a deep spiritual motif in almost all religions. Hindu theology, for example, has a particular word for this sudden, all-transforming glance: *darshan*. Whole treatises and spiritual disciplines within Hinduism exist to prepare devotees for the possibility of such an encounter and to help them deal with its all-altering consequences. Likewise, in Buddhism, with its tradition of wordless communication, the direct pointing to reality, the *locus classicus* is the so-called 'Flower Sermon', in which the Buddha held up a flower and the particular disciple who met his gaze and gazed with him on the flower attained enlightenment in that single glance. Tradition has it that this disciple subsequently brought Buddhism to China and thus became the first patriarch of Zen. This same motif, though perhaps more deeply hedged about with a sense of awe, wonder and fear, is also found in the Judaeo-Christian tradition. But here a tragic element of lostness, elegy and longing is introduced. The Hebrew scriptures begin, as it were, with an original blessing, an 'originall joy' as Herbert calls it, in which God and humanity walk together in the garden in the cool of the evening, naturally and without shadow, face to face.

The tragedy of the fall breaks that; the mutual openness of the
exchanged glance is lost, replaced by obfuscation and hiding. 'He
said, "I heard the sound of you in the garden, and I was afraid,
because I was naked; and I hid myself"' (Genesis 3.10). Yet God
seeks the hidden Adam, that the shame-faced may be face to face
again. This tension between hiding and full-faced encounter runs
deeply through the entire Old Testament. 'No one shall see me
and live,' says Yahweh to Moses (Exodus 33.20). But the psalmist
says,

> 'Come,' my heart says, 'seek his face!'
> Your face, LORD, do I seek.
> (Psalm 27.8)

The vision is forbidden and yet the vision is the deepest thing
we long for. We yearn for that of which we are rightly afraid.
So when Isaiah, in the year that King Uzziah died, sees the Lord
lifted up he cannot bear the vision and cries, 'Woe is me!' (Isaiah
6.5). Christmas, to which we look forward in this season, is the
central and reconciling event that comes into being and takes its
meaning within this field of tension, between hiding and seeking.
The first thing that John the Evangelist wants to say after he has
proclaimed the essential Christmas gospel, that 'the Word was
made flesh', is not that we have speculated upon his nature but
'we beheld his glory' (John 1.14, AV). Indeed, in that first chapter
John goes on to tell the story that is almost certainly the subtext
and context for Herbert's beautiful poem: the story of Nathanael.

As the disciples begin to gather around Jesus, Philip finds
Nathanael and says, 'We have found him, of whom Moses in
the law, and the prophets, did write, Jesus of Nazareth, the son
of Joseph' (John 1.45, AV). Nathanael's unpromising response is
'Can anything good come out of Nazareth?' But Philip gives the
best reply that anyone sharing the mystery of their faith could
give: 'Come and see.' That 'come and see' sets a theme of 'seeing'
and vision, which culminates in the amazing exchange between
Nathanael and Jesus that follows (John 1.47–51).

Before Nathanael has uttered a word, Jesus says, 'Behold an
Israelite indeed', and turns the tables of 'vision' onto Nathanael

himself; in that moment Nathanael suddenly knows that he is completely known by this man he has never met. 'Whence knowest thou me?' he asks, and Jesus' reply is again about vision and seeing: 'Before that Philip called thee, when thou wast under the fig tree, I saw thee.' Something amazing happens here. Nathanael, who was scoffing at Nazareth a minute before, has a sudden leap of understanding, outpacing reason or teaching, overtaking all the other disciples to an understanding and certainty that even Peter would not attain for another three years. He declares, 'Rabbi, thou art the Son of God; thou art the King of Israel.' Something whole and complete has been disclosed in a single glance; to see and to be seen is enough! Here in the Gospel is a sudden 'awakening', a direct pointing to reality, such as we noticed with Hinduism and Buddhism.

So we can see that Herbert's particular and personal experience recorded in this poem is a deep part of the wider spiritual tradition he inhabits, but it is nevertheless still personal; it is not Christ's glance on Nathanael but Love, 'quick-eyed Love', as he later calls him, looking straight into the heart of the poet. Tradition is the nurturing ground and overarching frame that makes certain experiences possible and allows us to interpret them, but we must still seek to have the experience ourselves. The mediation and imaginative reach of poetry like this may well be one way in which the wider experience can become personally ours. Let's look in detail at what else is happening in this poem.

This first glance into Herbert's soul is at once unexpected and undeserved. Herbert is in the midst of youth and night; by his own account he is 'weltring in sinne'. But the sudden glance of Love transforms all, not by desert, but by sheer grace. It is as if in his text we can hear Paul's undersong: 'while we were yet sinners, Christ died for us ... when we were enemies, we were reconciled to God' (Romans 5.8, 10, AV). Herbert touches on an essential experience here, not only specifically but in the realm of human love and a sudden exposure to undeserved love. To know that someone looks on us and sees good where perhaps we have seen only 'night' and 'weltring sinne' is in itself transformative. Herbert, in a beautiful, itself 'overrunning' line, speaks of how delight at this unexpected glance comes to

Bedew, embalme, and overrunne my heart,
And take it in

drawing an even deeper sense from the word 'cordial'. Both
the language and the experience of the glance that suddenly
makes you overflow with love and grace is strongly reminiscent
of Dante's account of his meeting in the marketplace when he
received Beatrice's 'salute', a word which plays on both salutation
and salvation:

> I say that when she appeared in any place, it seemed to me,
> by the hope of her excellent salutation, that there was no man
> mine enemy any longer; and such warmth of charity came upon
> me that most certainly in that moment I would have pardoned
> whosoever had done me an injury; and if one should then have
> questioned me concerning any matter, I could only have said
> unto him 'Love,' with a countenance clothed in humbleness.
> (Dante Alighieri, *La Vita Nuova* XI, p. 46)

Herbert's phrase 'And take it in' is worth pausing upon. It does
not, of course, carry anything of the modern sense of 'being taken
in', of 'being deceived'. On the contrary, it is an allusion to the
hospitality of taking in a guest. It may be a direct echo of Jesus'
words, 'I was a stranger and you took me in' (Matthew 25.35),
but here it is not Herbert who takes in Christ, but Christ who in
one glance takes Herbert's heart into his own. Now the three-
verse form of the poem comes into its own: the first looks back to
the first glance, the third looks forward to 'full-ey'd love'; and the
second meditates on how the memory of the first glance can sus-
tain us now. Herbert candidly admits that even the most profound
spiritual experience in no way shields us from bitterness, pain or
malice, from what, in a telling phrase, he calls 'surging griefs',
but rather that spiritual experience, while not shielding us from
'the thousand natural shocks that flesh is heir to', is nevertheless
not overwhelmed by them. There is somewhere deep within us a
'sweet originall joy', which can, if we will let it, 'work' great good
within our souls. In the final stanza comes a great expression of

our Advent hope. Herbert opens with a beautiful piece of poetic reasoning:

If thy first glance so powerfull be,
A mirth but open'd and seal'd up again;
What wonders shall we feel, when we shall see
Thy full-ey'd love!

His beautiful phrase, 'A mirth but open'd and seal'd up again', is a rare example of the word 'mirth' being preceded by the indefinite article. Mirth is not some vague general state, but becomes a particular thing, like some closely guarded and precious scent, kept sealed in a bottle; opened for a minute, its perfume fills the room, full of promise, then sealed again, for a fuller day. And there is one final turn to this extraordinary poem. We are used to the idea of the beatific vision, the idea that simply to see and contemplate God represents complete satisfaction of every longing. While this is a true and beautiful thought, there is a danger, particularly with some of the more abstract and philosophical theologians, that this beatific vision can be seen almost as an intellectualized and impersonal contemplation of truth (the peculiar satisfaction of academics, rather than the deeper fulfilment of everyone's longings). In the last four lines of this poem, Herbert turns this around. For what we shall see is not an abstract condition or a blessed state, but 'full-ey'd love', and what full-eyed love does is to look back on us: to look us out of pain and into delight.

As we read this poem at the beginning of Advent, perhaps we can think of it like this. The coming of the Christ-child at Christmas is a first glance, 'A mirth but open'd'; and perhaps that mirth is in many ways sealed up again: the Christmas mirth put away when the decorations are taken down at Epiphany; the mirth of that child, delighting in his mother's arms, sealed in a stone-cold tomb. Perhaps the mirth and 'sugred strange delight' of our own first conversion may have been sealed up again. But even that small mirth has sustained us. Advent is the time when we look forward to the day when we shall see Christ's 'full-ey'd love'.

2 DECEMBER

The Moons *Grevel Lindop*

Too many moons to fill an almanac:
the half, the quarters, and the slices between
black new and silvercoin full –
pearl tossed and netted in webs of cloud,
thread of light with the dull disc in its loop,
gold shaving afloat on the horizon of harvest –
How many times did you call me from the house,
or from my desk to the window, just to see?
Should I string them all on a necklace for you?
Impossible, though you gave them all to me.
Still some of their light reflects from memory.
Here it is, distant gleam on the page of a book.

Yesterday we enjoyed, in 'The Glance', a poem about seeing, about the movement from a first glance to a full-eyed love. Today's poem is also about seeing, about glimpsing, indeed about stringing together many glimpses in an attempt to lift them from time on the thread of memory. But whereas yesterday's poem was by a clearly and explicitly Christian poet, bringing the full resources of his theology to bear on the meaning and, as it were, the eternal weight of glory in the glance he celebrates, today's poet does not share that cosmic reach of faith, though he does, like Herbert, reflect on how remembered glimpses enrich us now. Grevel Lindop, an accomplished contemporary poet, as well as fine essayist and travel writer, takes up an age-old and classic 'trope' of poetry, the sight of the moon, and makes new music with a quiet beauty. It seems to me that he gives expression to two of the deepest Advent themes: the passage of time, and the quality of light in darkness. For many poets the waxing and waning of the moon have been an emblem of mutability, transience and loss. Philip Sidney and Philip Larkin both saw her climb the heavens with 'sad steps'. But for Lindop the changing phases of the moon, 'the half, the quarters, and the slices between', are something to celebrate, each in its distinct beauty, strung on memory like beads on jewellery, evoked in words like 'silvercoin', 'pearl', 'thread of light', 'gold'. Then, on the seventh line, we realize that the poet is not watching the moon alone, but with someone, to whom the poem is addressed; indeed, he confesses that without that someone he would never have glimpsed the images he has just strung, netted in the webs of the poem, strung on the thread of light which is language. He wants to offer them as a gift to the one who called him to see them, but knows he can never fully do this:

Should I string them all on a necklace for you?
Impossible, though you gave them all to me.

Instead he offers her the poem itself, and in a beautiful turn, even the white page of the book in which the poem is printed seems to reflect the remembered moonlight:

Still some of their light reflects from memory.
Here it is, distant gleam on the page of a book.

Of course, the frame of this poem is well within this world: glimpses and glances of what Coleridge movingly called 'the moving moon' offered to a companion in the darkness of our common journey. But by reading this poem now, close to the beginning of the 'thread of light' that draws us through Advent, I would like to suggest another way we might reframe it. It may be a friend or a lover who encourages us to leave our desk or house to glimpse the moon, but might we not also feel that through that friend, through the gift of our eyes and vision, through the very framing of the heavens, it is also God who calls us. 'Come and look at this – it's beautiful'; 'The heavens are telling the glory of God; and the firmament proclaims his handiwork. Day to day pours forth speech, and night to night declares knowledge' (Psalm 19.1–2); 'The people who walked in darkness have seen a great light; those who dwelt in a land of deep darkness – on them light has shined' (Isaiah 9.2). The poet wants to respond to the gift of these glimpses, to offer them back to the giver, strung like pearls, and offers her instead the only gift he has – the poem. Might we not do the same for the giver behind these gifts, the Light who made light, to whom we too can say, 'you gave them all to me'?

Advent is the time when we move from glimpses of that giver from afar, like the distant moon and stars, to the astonishing realization that the one we glimpsed is coming close to us, to meet us with his 'full-ey'd love'.

3 DECEMBER

Annunciation *John Donne*

Salvation to all that will is nigh;
That All, which always is all everywhere,
Which cannot sin, and yet all sins must bear,
Which cannot die, yet cannot choose but die,
Lo! faithful Virgin, yields Himself to lie
In prison, in thy womb; and though He there
Can take no sin, nor thou give, yet He'll wear,
Taken from thence, flesh, which death's force may try.
Ere by the spheres time was created thou
Wast in His mind, who is thy Son, and Brother;
Whom thou conceivest, conceived; yea, thou art now
Thy Maker's maker, and thy Father's mother,
Thou hast light in dark, and shutt'st in little room
Immensity, cloister'd in thy dear womb.

Today's poem, on the mystery of the Annunciation, is the first
of several that focus on Mary's unique and beautiful role in the
advent of Christ and are interspersed throughout this Advent
sequence. Although her role as *Theotokos*, the God-bearer, is in
one way unique, in that she alone physically nurtures and brings
into the world the body and person of Jesus Christ, in another way
Mary is the archetype of every Christian soul, and of the whole
Church. We are all in some way called to respond to God's prom-
ise, to say 'be it unto me according to thy word' (Luke 1.38, AV),
to treasure his words and the gift of his spirit in our hearts, and
in some way even in the intimacy of our own flesh and daily lives,

to bear him into the world. In all these things Mary is our model and our encouragement, particularly in Advent when in various ways we prepare both outwardly and visibly and inwardly and spiritually for his 'arrival' at Christmas. Reflecting on the intensity with which a woman in late pregnancy prepares for the birth of her child can be immensely helpful for us. So in one sense the Annunciation has its own proper season in the spring; in another, Advent is itself the call to respond to an Annunciation.

In the Introduction to this book, I spoke of the spiritual and literary tradition that nurtured and framed the work of writers like George Herbert and Christina Rossetti, a tradition mediated not only in general terms by a wider culture but directly and intimately from one person to another. George Herbert's 'The Glance' (1 December) is part of this tradition, and today's poet, John Donne, Herbert's older contemporary, was indeed a personal mediator and transmitter of the tradition to the younger poet. Donne was a member of a circle of wits, scholars and poets who gathered around Herbert's brilliant mother, Magdalen, and this poem on the Annunciation was part of a sequence called 'La Corona'[1] that was in fact sent by Donne as a personal gift to Herbert's mother. The poems may well have arisen not only from personal meditation and devotion but from intense personal conversation with Magdalen, and some scholars think that this accounts for the space, attention and honour that Donne pays

---

1 La Corona is an interesting and ambiguous title for this poetic sequence. It is a corona or 'crown' in the sense that the sonnets are interwoven in a circle. The last line of one sonnet becomes the first line of the next, the last line of the final poem being the first line of the opening one. In that sense, the whole sequence has a womb-like circularity containing its own immensities. But there was another extant meaning of the word 'corona', one that was for Donne more dangerous. The corona was a Dominican variation on the rosary, and a smaller sequence of said 'Hail Marys', Annunciations, each of which contained a meditation on one of the mysteries of faith. And that is what Donne's 'Corona' is intended to be: a linked sequence of seven meditations on the great mysteries of faith from the Annunciation to the Ascension. While the outward and visible meditation aid of the rosary beads was forbidden at that time, Donne transfigured them, protecting their essence as innocent sonnets.

to the feminine. Like all Donne's poetry, this little sonnet on the Annunciation is richly and densely packed, as befits a poem whose ringing final line speaks of 'Immensity, cloister'd'. Let us try and open some of the riches Donne has shut in this 'little room'.

'Annunciation' does indeed start with an enunciation, but not the one we are expecting. Not the individual and particular 'Hail Mary, full of grace, the Lord is with thee', but something addressed more directly to all of us: 'Salvation to all that will is nigh', the quintessential Advent proclamation that 'now is our salvation nearer than when we believed' (Romans 13.11, AV). But Donne has no sooner made this universal proclamation in which the little word 'all' includes every one of us than he takes the same small word, capitalizes it, and suddenly it also stands for the immensity and mystery of an infinite God. Evoked in the second line, 'That All, which always is all everywhere', the dry, abstract, doctrinal word 'omnipresent' is suddenly made richly and mellifluously simple. As Donne himself put it in one of his sermons, God is 'replenishingly everywhere'. But now, having established this 'allness everywhere', Donne brings us sharply to the paradox that 'All everywhere' has become particularly this tiny seed in the womb. In some ways, Donne's exuberant and paradoxical love poetry was a *praeparatio evangelica* for the greater paradox of his faith. In 'The Sun Rising' he spoke of how the sheer concentration of erotic love could make 'one little room an everywhere'. Here he takes these phrases from his earlier poem – 'little room' and 'everywhere' – and brings them to bear on the mystery of Christ's coming in flesh. In this sonnet, the paradoxes are packed ever more closely together, that 'All' which is God is one

> Which cannot sin, and yet all sins must bear,
> Which cannot die, yet cannot choose but die.

Then, at the fifth line, the sonnet takes a daring turn. Donne was writing in a fervently Protestant country; prayers to the Virgin or direct religious invocation of her were banned. The drive to 'unmask' an alleged Jesuitical 'fifth column' divided families, and unguarded remarks or turns of phrase could cause suspicion. But

Donne, perhaps inspired by the patronage and guardianship of Herbert's devout mother, nonetheless addresses the rest of the poem directly to Mary:

> Lo! faithful Virgin, yields Himself to lie
> In prison, in thy womb

As he does so, he goes out of his way to emphasize Mary's vital role in giving Christ flesh in the cloister of her womb. The lines speaking of Christ actually taking flesh are particularly telling, but also very dense and perhaps in need of some explication:

> He'll wear,
> Taken from thence, flesh, which death's force may try.

That is to say, the flesh Christ will wear is taken directly from Mary's womb, and that flesh, like all flesh, is on a collision course with death. But the phrase that tells us that flesh 'death's force may try' is deliberately ambiguous. We can take it to mean that the force of death will 'try' Christ's flesh, which indeed it does as he suffers the terrible death on the cross. But it could equally mean that Christ's flesh will 'try' the force of death itself: bring it to trial, to battle, to the test as to whether death is absolute or not. And this, of course, is precisely what Christ came to do, destroying, in his own death, death itself, so that death is swallowed up in victory. And this paradox is a theme in Donne's later devotional poetry (for 'La Corona' is perhaps as early as 1607), in poems like 'Death be not Proud'.

In the sestet of this sonnet – at the turn, or *volta*, which so often establishes a new theme or motif – he sets the intimate particularity of her womb and flesh in a cosmic and eternal context, and in a brilliant image sees the Virgin Mary already radiant in the mind of the Logos who was to become her son before time has even begun:

> Ere by the spheres time was created thou
> Wast in His mind, who is thy Son, and Brother

Pressing the paradox further, Donne plays upon the twin senses of the word 'conceive', at once metaphysical and physical; and this desire to use 'conceive' both for eternal thought and for the temporal event in the womb is itself a mimesis or model of incarnation, and of Christ's double nature – both God and man in one person, 'Whom thou conceivest, conceived'. Now Donne draws deeper still from an older Catholic tradition and makes his own playful reworking of the hymn to Mary that Dante put in the mouth of Bernard of Clairvaux. Bernard calls Mary '*figlia del tuo filio*', 'daughter of thy son'. This phrase struck T. S. Eliot so deeply that he quoted it verbatim in *The Four Quartets* ('The Dry Salvages' IV). Donne's take on it drives the paradoxes even further: 'Thy Maker's maker, and thy Father's mother'. The final couplet brings us an image that is again central to our Advent meditations: the light that shines in darkness. There is something fitting in Donne's choice of the sonnet, one of the most compressed and concentrated of poetic forms, with which to deal with the mystery of compression and particularity, and indeed he wittily alludes to that, for the word 'stanza' (for a verse of poetry) means 'little room' in Italian. In one sense, he is directly praising the Virgin for having the light of Christ in the darkness of her womb:

Thou hast light in dark, and shutt'st in little room
Immensity, cloister'd in thy dear womb.

But in another sense, Mary's making becomes a model for Donne's own poetic endeavour as he too shuts, within the little room of his sonnet, mysteries to which we can return, and which will continually open for his readers.

4 DECEMBER

Annunciation *Scott Cairns*

Deep within the clay, and O my people
very deep within the wholly earthen
compound of our kind arrives of one clear,
star-illumined evening a spark igniting
once again the tinder of our lately
banked noetic fire. She burns but she
is not consumed. The dew lights gently,
suffusing the pure fleece. The wall comes down.
And – *do you feel the pulse?* – we all become
the kindled kindred of a King whose birth
thereafter bears to all a bright nativity.

Yesterday we considered a densely packed poem on the mystery
of the Annunciation by a seventeenth-century master seeking
to compress the immensity of this event into the 'little room' of
his sonnet. Today, we look into another brief meditation on the
same mystery, this time by a contemporary poet, Scott Cairns, an
American Greek Orthodox. He has been crafting a body of work
that is both completely modern, full of the particularities of the
here and now, and also traditional, drawing richly on the liturgy,
theology and deep understanding of archetype and symbol that
are part of his Orthodox inheritance. He shares with John Donne
the ability to compress thought and feeling together, to juxtapose
the disparate, to rekindle an old image or metaphor until it burns
for us entirely new. 'Annunciation' is the penultimate poem in a
recent and most remarkable collection, *Idiot Psalms*. The poems

in this collection range widely through our human experience: glimpses of fields of arctic ice from an aeroplane window; sharing of succulent food in a Greek café; cries of anguish at the idiotic iteration of banal evil; moments of sheer and lucid transfiguration. And illuminating all of these are the sudden vertical lights of a deeply integrated faith and theology.

This poem can, of course, be read and enjoyed without any special commentary. Its suggestive clusters of words arising from notions of light and heat bring their own message as we read it in the cold and dark of December: 'star-illumined ... spark igniting ... noetic fire ... She burns ... lights gently ... kindled kindred ... bright nativity'. But there is a beautifully allusive spirit at play in this poem, and opening some of these allusions can deepen our response. The opening phrases

Deep within the clay, and O my people
very deep within the wholly earthen
compound of our kind

take us back to our beginnings in Genesis, to humanity formed from the clay of the earth by the God who delights to make each 'according to its *kind*' (Genesis 1). Cairns' lovely phrase, 'the wholly earthen compound of our kind', is a rich development of the Genesis image, suggesting the fact that we are 'compounded' of many things, and especially of body and spirit, earth and fire; it also summons, in 'wholly earthen', the almost elegiac Pauline phrase, 'But we have this treasure in clay jars' (2 Corinthians 4.7). The biblical and poetic echoes are deepened further in that first line by the vocative 'O my people'. Here, Cairns not only summons the direct echo of Micah, 'O my people, what have I done to you?' (Micah 6.3), but is also perhaps nodding to his poetic predecessor T. S. Eliot's use of the same line in 'Ash Wednesday': 'O my people, what have I done unto thee'. In both those cases, the context is one of reproach. What gives Cairns' use of the phrase a particular grace and power is that in his poem, 'O my people' begins the annunciation of good news; whatever evil we have done to God, in this annunciation he is coming deep within our 'wholly earthen compound' to do us good.

Then we come to the main verb of this first sentence: 'arrives'. Advent is a season that looks for a coming, for an arrival, and 'arrives', in that present continuous tense, sees its fulfilment. And what arrives is 'a spark igniting once again'. The Incarnation that begins with this annunciation to Mary is about arriving once again at the place where we started, the wholly good, original blessing of that Genesis moment evoked by the poem's opening. Something that has dimmed and nearly faded in us is being kindled again: 'the tinder of our lately banked noetic fire'.

There is something very beautiful and nuanced about the theology of fall and redemption offered here. Cairns is recognizing what has been lost in the fall, in our disobedience and falling away from our divine origin, but he resists the more extreme Protestant idea that the divine image, that holy spark, is utterly overthrown and extinguished in us, that in our fall we are completely and utterly depraved and without divine light. Instead, he offers the image of a banked fire, a curiously providential and redemptive idea in that the same matter that seems to smother the flames is allowing them to recover and continue. And what are we to make of this word 'noetic'? Its roots are in the Greek word for 'mind'; the very spark and light of our reason, *nous*, is a quality we share with the divine, with the eternal Logos who is the 'true light' that enlightens everyone who comes into the world (John 1.9), however much that inner light is obscured or banked by our fall. And in the coming of the Divine, a tiny spark deep in the clay of Mary's body, the body of all humanity, the divine *nous* burns again in us.

Then the poem turns to focus on Mary herself, the new Eve, and again by means of a deft and rich allusion to the scriptures: 'She burns but she is not consumed.' Suddenly we see the burning bush, to which Moses turned, standing barefoot on holy ground (Exodus 3.1–22), as the 'Type' of Mary, the *Theotokos*, the God-bearer, fully and wholly herself and yet bearing in herself and for us all our God. Cairns then turns from one patristic symbol of Mary to another: Gideon's fleece (Judges 6.36–40). The dew falling on Gideon's fleece alone, as a confirmation of the truth of God's word, becomes a type or sign of God's coming to us through Mary's prayerful 'Yes'. There may also be an echo here of the early English hymn 'I syng of a mayden':

> He came al so still
> Where his mother was
> As dew in April
> That falleth on the grass.

And this is all expressed in beautiful English poetry, particularly the lovely combination of alliteration and assonance in the phrase 'suffusing the pure fleece'. But there is more. The next phrase, 'The wall comes down', is given a sentence to itself, and is a great example of that technique of allusion, paradox and compression that Cairns shares with Donne. One sense of the wall coming down is clearly suggested by the allusion to Gideon and the fleece, and we think of trumpets and the wall of Jericho, and the way made open, this time by the trumpet of annunciation. The dark walls of our banked clay fall before the returning divine spark; and, of course, Gideon's men kept their torches under clay jars. But this is also another wall. Why did Jesus come? That he might break down 'the dividing wall' (Ephesians 2.14), the wall that divides us both from God and from one another. And this image of division overcome, humanity brought together by the one who has brought down the wall, is taken up in the turn at the last three lines, moving from 'you' to 'we':

> we all become
> the kindled kindred of a King whose birth
> thereafter bears to all a bright nativity.

And here again Cairns makes full use of the linguistic resources at a poet's disposal: the music in his phrase 'the kindled kindred of a King', the delicate play on 'birth' and 'bears', and the stunning final phrase, 'a bright nativity'. There is indeed immensity cloistered in these eleven lines.

5 DECEMBER

Those Winter Sundays *Robert Hayden*

Sundays too my father got up early
and put his clothes on in the blueblack cold,
then with cracked hands that ached
from labor in the weekday weather made
banked fires blaze. No one ever thanked him.

I'd wake and hear the cold splintering, breaking.
When the rooms were warm, he'd call,
and slowly I would rise and dress,
fearing the chronic angers of that house,

Speaking indifferently to him,
who had driven out the cold
and polished my good shoes as well.
What did I know, what did I know
of love's austere and lonely offices?

If Scott Cairns' 'Annunciation' ranged across the length and
breadth of scripture, and from a tiny spark on earth out to the
furthest star, this poem by contrast keeps us hunkered down and
focused on the small fires of a poor house in the dawn of a Detroit
winter Sunday. Robert Hayden (1913–80) was brought up in an
impoverished household in an African-American district where
his father worked for a pittance as a manual labourer. It was not
an easy childhood, and the house was filled with the tension of a
breaking marriage and the suppressed anger that so often accom-

panies oppression. Hayden alludes to this in 'fearing the chronic angers of that house'. So this is no cosy, nostalgic and retrospective romanticizing of poverty in the manner of Hovis television adverts. And it is for this very reason that we can credit the depth and reality of the hidden and practical love, in spite of all, to which this poem witnesses. Let's look at it in closer detail.

The language of this poem is essentially clear, simple, limpid. It does not draw attention to itself or to its own technique; nevertheless, the poem is very carefully and beautifully constructed. In the opening line, 'Sundays too my father got up early', everything is disclosed in that little word 'too': a quiet, understated way of telling us of his father's daily toil, Monday to Saturday, up early labouring for others. We see that, to serve his family, he does not permit himself Sunday as a day of rest. So we are prepared in that one word 'too' to meet 'the cracked hands that ached from labor in the weekday weather'. While the poem is apparently, if we just scan the end words, written in blank verse, Hayden in fact avails himself of the many rich possibilities arising from assonance and internal rhyme. There is effectively a rhyme structure, but it is hidden, serving the poem secretly; this is a perfect mimesis in the poem's form, of the hidden service that is the poem's subject. So, we have 'blueblack cold' echoing onto 'cracked hands', 'labor', 'day' and 'made' linking across the fourth line, and 'banked' and 'thanked' working together in the fifth line, all effectively intensifying our experience of the language, but quietly. This sense of the unthanked or hidden service is also emphasized by the contrast between the cold Hayden's father must endure as he labours in the weekday weather and the warmth that his extra Sunday labour leaves for his son.

The first verse focuses on the father, the second on the son as a child, and the third on both: now the son, old enough to be a father himself, looks back and sees at last what his father has done for him. The sense of the cold is beautifully conveyed in the line 'the cold splintering, breaking', with its stuttering consonantal feel, contrasted immediately with the easy, flowing, 'When the rooms were warm, he'd call'. But there is more going on in the language used to describe this father's unthanked, loving labour, something redemptive. This is a house full of fearful 'chronic angers'. All the words used to describe the father's labour and its effect, 'cracked', 'blaze', 'splintering', 'breaking', could describe what might happen if anger blazed out, if peace were splintered, if tempers, or even bodies, were to break. Like the fires, though, the anger is banked, and becomes part of the energy with which this father, instead of blazing out in temper, splintering or breaking his family, splinters and breaks the wood, and makes the 'banked fires blaze'.

Amid the intense contrasts there's something very powerful about the understated and matter-of-fact way in which Hayden records and confesses the indifference with which in those days he met this service: 'No one ever thanked him'; 'Speaking indifferently to him'. And this makes the extraordinary and memorable turn in the last two lines of the poem all the more poignant and effective:

What did I know, what did I know
of love's austere and lonely offices?

Here the language lifts and the very register changes. The lilting, almost liturgical repetition of the self-searching question, 'what did I know,' prepares us for the elevation and universal reach of the final line: 'love's austere and lonely offices'. It is almost as if the angry, labouring African-American in the blueblack cold of Detroit is glimpsed suddenly as an avatar of Love himself, or as some mystic or religious giving glory to God in the high austerity of monastic offices – the *opus dei*, the work of God. It's almost as though we see, for a moment, as in the old Benedictine dictum *laborare est orare*, work becoming prayer. And there is one final and telling paradox. Ostensibly, the last two lines are a confession of ignorance, an unawareness of 'love's austere and lonely offices'. But in the very act of confessing his childhood ignorance and indifference, the adult poet is becoming fully and thankfully aware; and through his poem he makes us aware too, not only of the working of love in this particular instance, but, as we lift our eyes from the page and think of all who serve us silently today, even before we wake, of 'love's austere and lonely offices' in our lives.

6 DECEMBER

From **The Ballad of the White Horse** G. K. *Chesterton*

And well may God with the serving-folk
Cast in His dreadful lot;
Is not He too a servant,
And is not He forgot?

For was not God my gardener
And silent like a slave;
That opened oaks on the uplands
Or thicket in graveyard gave?

And was not God my armourer,
All patient and unpaid,
That sealed my skull as a helmet,
And ribs for hauberk made?

Did not a great grey servant
Of all my sires and me,
Build this pavilion of the pines,
And herd the fowls and fill the vines,
And labour and pass and leave no signs
Save mercy and mystery?

For God is a great servant,
And rose before the day,
From some primordial slumber torn;
But all we living later born

Sleep on, and rise after the morn,
And the Lord has gone away.

On things half sprung from sleeping,
All sleeping suns have shone,
They stretch stiff arms, the yawning trees,
The beasts blink upon hands and knees,
Man is awake and does and sees –
But Heaven has done and gone.

For who shall guess the good riddle
Or speak of the Holiest,
Save in faint figures and failing words,
Who loves, yet laughs among the swords,
Labours, and is at rest?

But some see God like Guthrum,
Crowned, with a great beard curled,
But I see God like a good giant,
That, labouring, lifts the world.

It's possible that Robert Hayden may have become aware of
Chesterton's great poem *The Ballad of the White Horse* when he
was working with W. H. Auden. But whether or not he knew it,
the passage that we read today takes up the same motif of early
morning, unthanked service with which Hayden dealt yesterday,
but sets it in another and heavenly key. This passage comes at a
point in Book IV of the poem when the fugitive King Alfred is at
his lowest ebb. He appears at the edges of a fire where a woman
is preparing cakes, and she takes him for 'a beggar, such as lags
looking for crusts and ale'. She takes pity on him and asks him to
serve her by watching the fire:

There is a cake for any man
If he will watch the fire.

Left to himself, the king meditates on the fact that he has become the least of serving men, and suddenly realizes that his God has done the same.

> Is not He too a servant,
> And is not He forgot?

Then comes a series of wonderful verses in which creation itself is seen as the constant service of an unthanked and anonymous servant God, appearing first as gardener, then as armourer, as herder for the fowls, and worker among the vines. Chesterton was, of course, writing when not only the upper classes but most English middle-class families had servants. Most of his readers were people who awoke to fires that were already lit, rooms already swept, tables already laid. But, unlike many of his contemporary writers, Chesterton also numbered among his readers some of the servants who had to get up early to light these fires and sweep these rooms and lay these tables. He was popular in a similar way and among the same vast range of people that Dickens had been in his day. Indeed, this particular poem was often found in the kit bags or uniform pockets of ordinary private soldiers in World War One, when their bodies were brought away from the battlefields. So there is not only poignancy and theological truth but sharp social comment in the verse:

> For God is a great servant,
> And rose before the day,
> From some primordial slumber torn

Most of us could no longer be accused of taking our servants for granted, but this poem still gives us a double challenge. The ones who serve us, who prepare our ready-meals, sew our clothes, light our fires – not by kneeling on our own hearths but by drilling and toiling in danger for the oil we burn, or working all day in factories and packing plants – these people are even more ignored and unthanked than the domestic servants of Edwardian Britain. For we have outsourced their labour, that we might keep them at a convenient distance, and so not be confronted by their humanity. As we begin, through Advent, to make the many purchases that seem to be a necessary prelude to Christmas, it may be that this poem will prompt us to remember to give thanks and to pray for the 'great grey servant(s)' who have put these goods in our hands. The second challenge is, of course, to remember God himself, the great servant who is continually about 'love's austere and lonely offices' on our behalf: 'who, though he was in the form of God, did not regard equality with God as something to be exploited, but emptied himself, taking the form of a slave, being born in human likeness. And being found in human form, he humbled himself and became obedient to the point of death – even death on a cross' (Philippians 2.6–8).

7 DECEMBER

From **An Hymne of Heavenly Love** *Edmund Spenser*

Out of the bosome of eternall blisse,
In which He reigned with His glorious Syre,
He downe descended, like a most demisse
And abiect thrall, in fleshes fraile attyre,
That He for him might pay sinne's deadly hyre,
And him restore unto that happie state
In which he stood before his haplesse fate.

In flesh at first the guilt committed was,
Therefore in flesh it must be satisfyde;
Nor spirit, nor angel, though they man surpas,
Could make amends to God for man's misguyde,
But onely man himselfe, who selfe did slyde:
So, taking flesh of sacred virgin's wombe,
For man's deare sake He did a man become.

And that most blessed bodie, which was borne
Without all blemish or reprochfull blame,
He freely gave to be both rent and torne
Of cruell hands, who with despightfull shame
Revyling Him, that them most vile became,
At length Him nayled on a gallow-tree,
And slew the Just by most unjust decree.

O huge and most unspeakeable impression
Of Love's deep wound, that pierst the piteous hart

Of that deare Lord with so entyre affection,
And, sharply launcing every inner part,
Dolours of death into His soule did dart,
Doing him die that never it deserved,
To free His foes, that from His heast had swerved!

What hart can feel least touch of so sore launch,
Or thought can think the depth of so deare wound?
Whose bleeding sourse their streames yet never staunch,
But stil do flow, and freshly still redownd,
To heale the sores of sinfull soules unsound,
And clense the guilt of that infected cryme
Which was enrooted in all fleshly slyme.

O blessed Well of Love! O Floure of Grace!
O glorious Morning-Starre! O Lampe of Light!
Most lively image of thy Father's face,
Eternal King of Glorie, Lord of Might,
Meeke Lambe of God, before all worlds behight,
How can we Thee requite for all this good?
Or what can prize that Thy most precious blood?

Yet nought Thou ask'st in lieu of all this love,
But love of us, for guerdon of thy paine:
Ay me! what can us lesse than that behove?
Had He required life for us againe,
Had it beene wrong to ask His owne with gaine?
He gave us life, He it restored lost;
Then life were least, that us so little cost.

We concluded our reflections on Chesterton's poem yesterday
with those famous lines from Philippians about how Christ
'emptied himself, taking the form of a slave', humbling himself
and being obedient 'to the point of death – even death on a cross'.
This humble self-emptying is known as kenosis, after the Greek
word for 'emptied' in this text. Today and tomorrow we look at
poems that draw us into the mystery and meaning of kenosis, one

from the sixteenth century, the other from the twenty-first, both approaching the mystery with awe and wonder.

Today's poem is an extract from Edmund Spenser's much longer 'Hymne of Heavenly Love', which was originally published in *Fowre Hymns* in 1596, towards the end of his life. The whole poem runs to 287 lines and tells the story of God as Love: from the eternal exchange of Love in the Trinity, through the loving act of creating the cosmos to share love, and finally to the point where our extract starts, where Love, seeing the plight into which humankind has fallen, comes down from heaven to rescue us. The 'rhyme royal' form is borrowed from Chaucer, Spenser's great predecessor and model, and from Chaucer too comes the frankness, clarity and surprisingly 'ordinary' and secular language in which these holy mysteries are evoked. This beautiful passage, celebrating the heart of our faith, and linking the meaning of Christmas with the power of the Passion, deserves to be better known.

The opening lines have a wonderful force of alliteration, and the phrase for heaven, 'The bosome of eternal blisse', carries with it a sense of loving intimacy missing from the clichéd images of vast spaces of sky and golden harps. Then a direct contrast develops the 'taking the form of a slave' idea from Philippians:

He downe descended, like a most demisse
And abiect thrall, in fleshes fraile attyre

which forms a powerful juxtaposition with the opening lines. The next stanza summarizes the theological argument set out in Anselm's *Cur Deus Homo*: why our salvation can be achieved only by one who is both fully God and fully human. However, Spenser does not leave us long in theological abstraction but rather brings it home in the affecting line, 'For man's deare sake He did a man become'. Again, the third stanza works by means of powerful contrast and juxtaposition, this time contrasting Mary's tender care of the infant Christ with the hatred he meets at the cross; so we move from 'blessed bodie ... borne' to 'rent', 'torne', 'cruell', 'despightfull'. The couplet brings it home with language that could easily be from a popular ballad, rather than theological language:

> At length Him nayled on a gallow-tree,
> And slew the Just by most unjust decree.

The next two stanzas in this extract bring us into the picture; we move from the outward and visible action of the Passion (to put it paradoxically) to its inward and spiritual meaning, and in both stanzas this turns on the moment at which Christ's heart is pierced with the spear. What is really piercing Christ's heart, says Spenser, is love for us! He is wounded by love for us in our woundedness:

> O huge and most unspeakeable impression
> Of Love's deep wound, that pierst the piteous hart
> Of that deare Lord with so entyre affection,
> And, sharply launcing every inner part

I believe that this little-known passage is a source for three subsequent great moments in English poetry of the Passion. At the end of *The Tempest* Prospero asks to be set free by 'prayer which pierces so that it assaults mercy itself', where the piercing of God's heart of mercy becomes the point of liberation. In Herbert's poem 'Prayer' (see *The Word in the Wilderness*, p. 52), he summarizes all our prayer as 'Christ-side-piercing spear'; then in the *Four Quartets* Eliot takes up the idea that Christ's wounds are themselves the measure of the tender and healing compassion that also pierces us, as a surgeon might 'lance' a wound:

> The Wounded surgeon plies the steel
> That questions the distempered part
> Beneath the bleeding hands we feel
> The sharp compassion of the healer's art

Here Eliot is, I think, drawing on the very reversal and mirroring of which Spenser speaks: 'Love's deep wound' (a great phrase) is piercing Christ's heart, but immediately, in the next stanza, we are ourselves pierced and searched by it ('launch' means 'lance'), and that piercing is our healing:

What hart can feel least touch of so sore launch,
Or thought can think the depth of so deare wound?
Whose bleeding sourse their streames yet never staunch,
But stil do flow, and freshly still redownd,
To heale the sores of sinfull soules unsound

The next stanza reminds us again of who it is that suffers for us here, and so emphasizes kenosis again. It is the 'Eternal King of Glorie' who has become for us the 'Meeke lambe of God'. Tomorrow, we consider another reading of the mystery of kenosis, which also links a vivid sense of Christ's infancy with an anticipation of the Passion which is to come.

8 DECEMBER

Kenosis *Luci Shaw*

In sleep his infant mouth works in and out.
He is so new, his silk skin has not yet
been roughed by plane and wooden beam
nor, so far, has he had to deal with human doubt.

He is in a dream of nipple found,
of blue-white milk, of curving skin
and, pulsing in his ear, the inner throb
of a warm heart's repeated sound.

His only memories float from fluid space.
So new he has not pounded nails, hung a door,
broken bread, felt rebuff, bent to the lash,
wept for the sad heart of the human race.

The distinguished American poet Luci Shaw was born in 1928. She
is still writing great poetry, is the author of ten volumes of verse,
and is a moving force and inspiration for many of her younger
contemporaries, seeking to recover and express an imaginative
apprehension of the faith in North America. This poem is drawn
from her 2010 collection *Harvesting Fog*. The first thing that
strikes the reader is how delicately drawn and closely observed is
her description of the newborn Jesus:

In sleep his infant mouth works in and out.
He is so new, his silk skin has not yet
been roughed ...

I find this a very helpful corrective to certain classic portrayals of Mary and the infant Jesus in art and iconography, in which he so often appears as somehow already grown up: a little king, richly robed, sitting up on his mother's lap, haloed and dispensing blessings and wisdom! Instead, we get the detail of the 'infant mouth' working in and out, seeking the comfort of the breast. And this in itself conveys the kenosis perfectly. He is an infant; the Latin root of the word, *infans*, means, literally, 'without speech'. He will learn love first through touch and need and then later begin to drink in language with his mother's milk. And yet he is the Word, the Logos in whom and from whom all speech and meaning derive. Lancelot Andrewes (1555–1626), the great preacher and translator of the Authorized Version, marvelled at the same paradox, exclaiming, '*Verbum Infans*! The Word, without a word, The Word unable to speak a word,' a phrase Eliot famously took up in his own poetry. But then, like her predecessor Edmund Spenser, Shaw goes on to juxtapose and contrast this tender, fragile being, nestled into the love and warmth of his mother, with the coming of his manhood when his skin will be 'roughed by plane and wooden beam'; the plane alludes to his life as a carpenter, but the 'wooden beam', in powerful understatement, is a reference to the coming cross. This double theme – his making as a carpenter and our unmaking of him on the cross – continues in the final stanza:

> he has not pounded nails, hung a door,
> broken bread, felt rebuff, bent to the lash

Again, as with Spenser but in a much more contemporary resonance and cadence, the inner meaning of this outer suffering is presented in terms of Christ's entering into, and being pierced and hurt by, the suffering with which we all contend: 'human doubt' and 'the sad heart of the human race'. But all this is in the future, held in suspense, as it were, above the beautiful intimacy of mother and child so deftly evoked in the verse:

He is in a dream of nipple found,
of blue-white milk, of curving skin
and, pulsing in his ear, the inner throb
of a warm heart's repeated sound.

In one way the poem makes us feel for the infant Christ that poignant, almost elegiac compassion we have for any infant as we contemplate their vulnerable innocence and how hard, how rough, how dark is the world into which they are born. But here, as with Spenser, there is a beautiful reversal. With every other child it is we who feel the compassion and they who remain in impotent and blissful ignorance; in Shaw's last line, 'wept for the sad heart of the human race', we perceive something different. We realize that the one who weeps most deeply for the world is Christ himself, who comes to us in love; our healing and redemption will be found in the tears of his compassion.

9 DECEMBER

Old Age *Edmund Waller*

The seas are quiet when the winds give o'er;
So calm are we when passions are no more.
For then we know how vain it was to boast
Of fleeting things, so certain to be lost.
Clouds of affection from our younger eyes
Conceal that emptiness which age descries.

The soul's dark cottage, batter'd and decay'd,
Lets in new light through chinks that Time hath made:
Stronger by weakness, wiser men become
As they draw near to their eternal home.
Leaving the old, both worlds at once they view
That stand upon the threshold of the new.

A week ago, when we were considering Grevel Lindop's poem
'The Moons', we reflected on how both the inevitable passage of
time and the search for light in darkness are Advent themes that
are somehow underlined by the darkness of December and the
waning of the year. In some ways these themes are taken up in this
little piece by Edmund Waller. Waller (1606–87) was a poet who
anticipated the limpid, urbane, carefully wrought and polished
poetry in heroic couplets later brought to perfection by Pope and
Dryden. He lived through the trauma of the Civil War and was
imprisoned for his royalist sympathies; his best-known poem, 'Go
Lovely Rose', means that he is largely remembered as the arche-
typal poet of the *carpe diem*, the call to youth to seize the day and

37

enjoy the pleasures of life while they may. Both lover and beloved know only too well the truth of that poem's famous final couplet:

How small a part of time they share
That are so wondrous sweet and fair.

But 'Old Age', which transcends the merely sensuous, *memento mori*, 'come hither' poems of his youth, deserves to be better known. He deliberately set it as the last poem in his collected works, at the end of a long sequence of touching religious poems, giving it the rather awkward title 'On The Forgoing Divine Poems' (it was Arthur Quiller-Couch, when he was selecting and shortening it for an early twentieth-century edition of *The Oxford Book of English Verse,* who gave the poem its present title). So it has entered the canon in its present form, two gentle, reflective verses from the once-young cavalier poet on what it is to grow old. He is realistic about weakness, but not bitter or resentful; rather he sees in the calm, and even the melancholy, the sense of emptiness that sometimes comes with age, an opportunity for openness to God and for a new wisdom.

The first stanza gives us two rich and complementary images that become emblems of old age: the sea calming and the sky clearing. Yet here is also a note of sorrow and loss: the 'Clouds of affection' that impeded the clear judgement of our 'younger eyes' may have cleared; but at first, all we see, bleakly, is 'emptiness'. Taken by itself, 'Conceal the emptiness which age descries' would be a line worthy of Philip Larkin; and if Larkin had been writing this poem that's probably where he would have ended it. But, thankfully, Waller gives us a second and beautifully redemptive stanza, beginning with a memorable image:

The soul's dark cottage, batter'd and decay'd,
Lets in new light through chinks that Time hath made:

Here the darkness and difficulty of ageing – the emptiness, the sense of being battered and decayed – are fully and honestly acknowledged (this is no merely sentimental poem), but they are also transcended. The very weaknesses, decays and losses that age entails become, in Waller's wonderfully homely word, the 'chinks' that let in new light. I sometimes wonder if this couplet is not the source of Leonard Cohen's wonderful chorus in his song 'Anthem':

There is a crack in everything
That's how the light gets in.

Waller follows this with a little meditation on St Paul's teaching on strength and weakness in 2 Corinthians 12.10, that 'whenever I am weak, then I am strong'; also perhaps glancing at 2 Corinthians 4.16: 'So we do not lose heart. Even though our outer nature is wasting away, our inner nature is being renewed day by day':

Stronger by weakness, wiser men become
As they draw near to their eternal home.

He concludes the poem with the beautiful, numinous image of coming to a threshold between two worlds; he ends this meditation on growing old, and also his own body of writing, concluding on the last page of his last book with one uplifting word that embodies our Advent hope: 'new'!

10 DECEMBER

In drear nighted December *John Keats*

In drear nighted December,
  Too happy, happy tree,
Thy branches ne'er remember
  Their green felicity –
The north cannot undo them
With a sleety whistle through them
Nor frozen thawings glue them
  From budding at the prime.

In drear nighted December,
  Too happy, happy brook,
Thy bubblings ne'er remember
  Apollo's summer look;
But with a sweet forgetting,
They stay their crystal fretting,
Never, never petting
  About the frozen time.

Ah! would 'twere so with many
  A gentle girl and boy –
But were there ever any
  Writh'd not at passed joy?
The feel of not to feel it,
When there is none to heal it
Nor numbed sense to steel it,
  Was never said in rhyme.

Advent comes at a dark time of year, and included in this anthology are a number of poems that have helped me reflect on the season itself, on our common and, as it were, secular experience of the dark and cold, as the frame in which we remember and look forward to light and warmth – outward and visible as well as inward and spiritual. Keats' poem certainly gets the feel of the season, and lines from it often return to me on dark December nights with the wind in the trees. I want to summon the poem up now not simply to explicate or agree with it but to engage with it as a conversation partner as we meditate our Advent hope.

> In drear nighted December,
> Too happy, happy tree,
> Thy branches ne'er remember
> Their green felicity

Keats' felicitous phrase, 'drear nighted December', sums up the way many people feel in the dreary darkness of encroaching winter. But, much as I love his poetry, I think in this case Keats is wrong about the tree. Indeed, it is just because those bleak, rain-lashed December branches do 'remember their green felicity', and retain, hidden within themselves, the patterns and energy of their former green-ness, that they will unfold into leaf again in spring and be able, as Larkin said, of trees in May, to 'begin afresh, afresh, afresh'.

It can be the same with us: we manage to get through the winter, and also perhaps the severer seasons of the heart, because we carry the memories of spring; we are sustained by a kind of parley between memory and hope. So George Herbert, trying to cope with severe experiences of depression and loss, writes in his poem 'The Flower':

> Who would have thought my shrivel'd heart
> Could have recover'd greennesse? It was gone
> Quite under ground; as flowers depart
> To see their mother-root, when they have blown;
> Where they together

All the hard weather,
Dead to the world, keep house unknown.

But Herbert knew, even in the depth of winter, that

Grief melts away
Like snow in May,
As if there were no such cold thing.

And so in that great poem of recovery he writes:

And now in age I bud again,
After so many deaths I live ...

And what about us? We too, in 'drear nighted December', need to remember our 'green felicity', and surely that is just what we do in Advent, and in the whole approach to and celebration of Christmas. In the darkest time of the year Christ, the Life within us and the seed of light, is sown. The root of Jesse, the stock of that true vine from which we all spring, is planted in our hearts, just when our hearts may feel at their darkest and most ploughed up. So through the dark days of Advent I pray for him to come so deeply and quietly into our hearts that, as Lancelot Andrewes said, 'He may with one word make all green again'.

11 DECEMBER

Despised and Rejected *Christina Rossetti*

My sun has set, I dwell
In darkness as a dead man out of sight;
And none remains, not one, that I should tell
To him mine evil plight
This bitter night.
I will make fast my door
That hollow friends may trouble me no more.

'Friend, open to Me.' – Who is this that calls?
Nay, I am deaf as are my walls:
Cease crying, for I will not hear
Thy cry of hope or fear.
Others were dear,
Others forsook me: what art thou indeed
That I should heed
Thy lamentable need?
Hungry should feed,
Or stranger lodge thee here?

'Friend, My Feet bleed.
Open thy door to Me and comfort Me.'
I will not open, trouble me no more.
Go on thy way footsore,
I will not rise and open unto thee.

'Then is it nothing to thee? Open, see
Who stands to plead with thee.

Open, lest I should pass thee by, and thou
One day entreat My Face
And howl for grace,
And I be deaf as thou art now.
Open to Me.'

Then I cried out upon him: Cease,
Leave me in peace:
Fear not that I should crave
Aught thou mayst have.
Leave me in peace, yea trouble me no more,
Lest I arise and chase thee from my door.
What, shall I not be let
Alone, that thou dost vex me yet?

But all night long that voice spake urgently:
'Open to Me.'
Still harping in mine ears:
'Rise, let Me in.'
Pleading with tears:
'Open to Me that I may come to thee.'
While the dew dropped, while the dark hours were cold:
'My Feet bleed, see My Face,
See My Hands bleed that bring thee grace,
My Heart doth bleed for thee,
Open to Me.'

So till the break of day:
Then died away
That voice, in silence as of sorrow;
Then footsteps echoing like a sigh
Passed me by,
Lingering footsteps slow to pass.
On the morrow
I saw upon the grass
Each footprint marked in blood, and on my door
The mark of blood for evermore.

It sometimes happens that a single poem becomes generative of many more. Some aspect of the tone or the techniques used in an earlier poem summons and releases energies in later poets, opening possibilities, beginning and continuing a conversation. Readers may well be familiar with George Herbert's exquisite poem 'Love (III)', with which he concludes *The Temple*:

> Love bade me welcome. Yet my soul drew back
> Guilty of dust and sin.
> But quick-eyed Love, observing me grow slack
> From my first entrance in,
> Drew nearer to me, sweetly questioning,
> If I lacked any thing.

The beautiful exchange in this poem between the first-person narrating voice and the figure who is Christ although he is not named as such – in which a familiar secular situation, the question of how best to welcome a guest, is enriched and transformed by a series of quiet scriptural allusions through which the secular scenario suddenly becomes a paradigm of spiritual encounter – has given rise to a number of other great poems in the same mode: Derek Walcott's 'Love After Love' and Michael O'Siadhai's 'Courtesy' are two examples of contemporary re-settings of Herbert's poem. But this dark and painful poem by Christina Rossetti may also be indebted and alluding to Herbert's 'Love (III)'. Here the tables are turned, though, as in Advent they must be. In Herbert's poem we come to Christ at his bidding to sit and eat, but at Advent, Christ comes to us and the question is opened: will there be room at the inn, will *we* bid *him* 'sit and eat'? Rossetti's poem goes to the heart of things. You will see the common elements: the dialogue about hospitality with an unnamed person who is really Christ, the dense layers of scriptural allusion, the secular situation suddenly transfigured with religious meaning. But Rossetti turns it round. What if we are to be the host, and Christ the guest? What if we should be the quick-eyed and hospitable love and Christ be the one we should bid welcome? How might the dialogue go then, if we were truly honest?

In Rossetti's poem it is Christ who comes as a stranger to the door, and we who should bid him welcome; but we ourselves are damaged and wounded people, and we cannot rise to the challenge. This poem is therefore a good antidote to the rather too easy and mawkish sentimentality that can accrue in the build-up to Christmas. We all happily sing that we will welcome him into our hearts, without counting the cost or stopping to wonder whether there is anything we should be doing to prepare what Yeats called 'the foul rag and bone shop of the heart' before our guest arrives.

It may be helpful to open out some of the scriptural allusions that give this subtle poem its secret force. The title comes directly from Isaiah 53.3: 'He was despised and rejected ... we held him of no account.' So in one sense we already know through Isaiah who the stranger is, and his rejection by the narrator is foreshadowed. This at once increases the dramatic irony, but also awakens in us a kind of compassion for the one who is doing the rejecting, as well as for the rejected. Then the opening verse, echoing the words of Psalm 143.3–4 ('For the enemy has pursued me, crushing my life to the ground, making me sit in darkness like those long dead. Therefore my spirit faints within me; my heart within me is appalled'), establishes the plight and bitterness of the narrator; but the verse concludes with a curiously modern touch: 'That hollow friends may trouble me no more'. It would be some years before Eliot came to write 'The Hollow Men', but already Rossetti knows what it is to inhabit the weariness, emptiness and doubt these words express. Then comes the knock at the door, and again the language and the situation summon a certain scriptural echo, this time from Revelation 3.20 ('Listen! I am standing at the door, knocking; if you hear my voice and open the door, I will come in to you and eat with you, and you with me'). The turn of this verse, in the lines

Others were dear,
Others forsook me: what art thou indeed
That I should heed

raises an important and again characteristically modern issue about how faith is known and shared. In the end, everything depends on trustworthy human relationships. A person who has been damaged and betrayed in one set of 'horizontal' or secular relationships may be genuinely prevented from opening in the 'vertical' dimension to the Divine. This is why Christians, when sharing faith, must be sensitive to what words like 'father', 'brother', 'husband', when used of the Divine, may mean to the listener. The verse finishes as the narrator summons for the reader, but tragically not for herself, echoes of Matthew 25.35 ('for I was hungry and you gave me food, I was thirsty and you gave me something to drink, I was a stranger and you welcomed me'). And so verse by verse it is as though there is an insistent double knocking: the outward and audible knock of the unknown stranger, and the constant beating upon us of powerful biblical reference opening up the true meaning, through to the echoes of Lamentations 1.12 that open the final stanza ('Is it nothing to you, all you who pass by? Look and see if there is any sorrow like my sorrow'). As the poem progresses, we learn more and more about the stranger at the door, and in the end this knowledge is concentrated into the five wounds of Christ:

'My Feet bleed, see My Face,
See My Hands bleed that bring thee grace,
My Heart doth bleed for thee,
Open to Me.'

But we are given the most important clue in the whole poem, indeed the key to understanding its ending, which is that there is grace in the blood: 'See My Hands bleed that bring thee grace'. Without this we might be tempted to stay on the surface with an untransfigured narrative, which is indeed one of despair, and to fear that the one who despised and rejected the stranger has in her turn been despised and rejected. But not so. The echo of the poem's final lines and rhyme changes everything:

and on my door
The mark of blood for evermore.

Here the most powerful and deeply submerged of the scriptural
allusions comes into play. For the blood on her door is the blood of
the lamb, and in another sense this night is Passover. The children
of Israel were saved by the blood on the lintel. In a poem that
has been unsparing in its insight into how bitterness and rejection
only beget more bitterness and rejection – a poem about a closed
door – Christina Rossetti nevertheless invites us in the last lines to
open a door to the possibility of salvation, even and especially for
the one who has most bitterly rejected the blood that saves her.

12 DECEMBER

In Memoriam XXVIII *Alfred Lord Tennyson*

The time draws near the birth of Christ:
  The moon is hid; the night is still;
  The Christmas bells from hill to hill
Answer each other in the mist.

Four voices of four hamlets round,
  From far and near, on mead and moor,
  Swell out and fail, as if a door
Were shut between me and the sound:

Each voice four changes on the wind,
  That now dilate, and now decrease,
  Peace and goodwill, goodwill and peace,
Peace and goodwill, to all mankind.

This year I slept and woke with pain,
  I almost wish'd no more to wake,
  And that my hold on life would break
Before I heard those bells again:

But they my troubled spirit rule,
  For they controll'd me when a boy;
  They bring me sorrow touch'd with joy,
The merry merry bells of Yule.

This is the first of two extracts in this anthology from Tennyson's masterpiece, *In Memoriam*. They are both about hearing church bells ring around Christmastide, but they could not be more different in tone, and their contrast frames and perhaps almost defines the whole movement and journey of the poem. Although not published until 1850, *In Memoriam* was begun in response to a tragic event in 1833, the early death of Tennyson's closest friend Arthur Henry Hallam. It takes the form of 131 poems, all written in the same closely controlled quatrain form, and composed gradually over several years as a kind of journal and outworking of grief towards recovery: of doubt and faith, of the loss and final restoration of vision. In the poem itself Tennyson described each of these brief lyrics as

> Short swallow-flights of song, that dip
> Their wings in tears, and skim away.
> (XLVIII)

It is a moving and searingly honest work in which Tennyson wrestles not only with personal grief and the doubt and despair occasioned by this tragedy, but with larger doubts about Christian faith in light of both the perennial problem of evil and the new findings of science that seemed to contradict Christian hope and confidence. It is from this poem that we draw the famous lines:

> There lives more faith in honest doubt,
> Believe me, than in half the creeds.
> (XCVI)

But it also contains, in the Prologue, this beautiful integration of faith, reason and humility:

> Our little systems have their day;
> They have their day and cease to be:
> They are but broken lights of thee,
> And thou, O Lord, art more than they.

> We have but faith: we cannot know;
> For knowledge is of things we see
> And yet we trust it comes from thee,
> A beam in darkness: let it grow.

Today's extract comes from early in the poem, when the pangs of grief are still new and raw; it deals with an experience that many readers will know and share, and may even be experiencing now: facing a first Christmas without the beloved. And I include this poem for that very reason.

It starts with a beautiful and seemingly peaceful evocation of the familiar sound of bells echoing from hill to hill: four church towers in four little hamlet parish churches in the Lincolnshire wolds, as they 'Answer each other in the mist'. The very sound of the bells echoing and returning to one another is evoked in the mirrored and enfolded repetition of the message he knows they are intended to bring:

Peace and goodwill, goodwill and peace,
Peace and goodwill, to all mankind.

What could be more peaceful, calm and reassuring than the nostalgic glow of this very English idyll? But all is not well, for the heart that hears the bells is numb with grief and shut out from joy; it is a heart that, as yet, has no peace. This sense of exclusion, occlusion, of something failing to reach him, is in fact delicately suggested, and the fuller confession of grief that is to come is anticipated in the very phrasing with which the bells are described, introducing at an almost unconscious level the language of loss and disconnection: 'hid ... mist ... fail ... as if a door were shut ...'

And then comes the breakdown, the sudden stab of bitterness and despair; grief attacks us even in the midst of, or perhaps because we are in the midst of, other people's peace and beauty:

This year I slept and woke with pain,
I almost wish'd no more to wake,
And that my hold on life would break
Before I heard those bells again:

There is such honesty in that confession of the death wish: a sense of how fragile is one's hold on life, with little will to go on, in that central couplet, turning on 'wake' and 'break', itself enclosed in the rhymes on 'pain' and 'again'. It is dreadful to experience these things, but I think a real strength and courage for facing them can be found from reading them in the experience of another. Tennyson's very effort to give this pain and doubt expression, and in such lucid form, is paradoxically an act of courage and resistance. It is courage and resistance that make possible the 'turn' in the final stanza of this section of the poem, which begins with the vital word 'But'. Here we are in the realm of those great moments in the Psalms, those laments that suddenly move from despair to hope: 'But I ... will praise thee' (Psalm 71.14); 'But you heard my supplications when I cried out to you' (Psalm 31.22). Tennyson returns to the sound of the bells that have awoken bitter grief, and lets their very music, and the memory it evokes, help him to control the grief:

> But they my troubled spirit rule,
> For they controll'd me when a boy

Somehow the bells have summoned, behind the memory of loss, deeper memories: of how the child's spirit lifted as he listened to the Christmas bells. The next line puts it beautifully: 'They bring me sorrow touch'd with joy'. The dominant note is still sorrow, but still, in spite of everything, it can be 'touch'd with joy'. For the rest of the work Tennyson takes the reader with him through the slow, delicate process of healing, until he can share with us a great affirmation of redemptive joy. The second, more famous account of hearing bells ring – 'Ring out, wild bells, to the wild sky' – will be our reading on New Year's Day.

13 DECEMBER

Launde Abbey on St Lucy's Day *Malcolm Guite*

St Lucy's day is brief and bright with frost,
In round cupped dew ponds shallow waters freeze,
Delicate fronds and rushes are held fast,
The low sun brings a contrast to the trees
Whose naked branches, dark against the skies
And fringed with glory by the light behind,
In patterns too severe for tired eyes,
Burn their bright image on the weary mind.
St Lucy's sun still bathes these abbey walls
And in her garden rose stalks stark and bare
Shine in a frosty light that yet recalls
The glory of the summer roses there.
Though winter night will soon surround us here,
Another Advent comes, Dayspring is near.

St Lucy's day, which falls today, used to be the winter solstice, before a change of calendars moved that to its more familiar position on 21 December. So it is quite understandable that an early Christian martyr, whose name means 'light', came to have her festivities at the solstice; and that we should seek to celebrate light on the briefest and darkest day. It is also not surprising that it is the most northern of European countries that make the most of St Lucy; many people will be familiar with the Scandinavian celebrations in which the eldest daughter of the family rises early, robed in white and with a crown of berries and lit candles on her head. She brings holiday food to her family while they sing

'Sankta Lucia', and thus the first celebration of the coming Christmas season is ushered in.

It is more surprising to see how this sense of contrast between darkness and light, and centred on the figure of St Lucy, survived even into Protestant England when so many saints' days and old ceremonies were abolished. But as late as 1612 Donne could write his strange love poem, possibly addressed to another Lucy, the Countess of Bedfordshire, 'A Nocturnal upon St Lucy's Day', with its haunting opening lines:

'Tis the year's midnight, and it is the day's,
Lucy's, who scarce seven hours herself unmasks;
The sun is spent, and now his flasks
Send forth light squibs, no constant rays;
The world's whole sap is sunk

Donne goes on to express the way many people feel around the shortest day of the year:

life is shrunk,
Dead and interr'd; yet all these seem to laugh,
Compared with me, who am their epitaph.

It is a day to admit those feelings, but also one on which to look for holy light, for Sankta Lucia.

It happened that on last St Lucy's day I was at Launde Abbey in Leicestershire, leading an Advent retreat based on the seven great 'O Antiphons'; I had written a sonnet sequence about them, and I share these later in this anthology. That day I got up early, just before sunrise. Launde is in its own little valley, a discrete dip or cup in the gentle folds of land there, and I witnessed the moment when the bright low sun emerged above the rim of that cup and suddenly bathed and blessed the old abbey walls, the bare winter trees and the bright ice on frozen dewponds, with glorious and somehow unexpected light. I walked in that light to the old rose garden (where the summer before, when roses were in bloom, I had composed sonnets for St Benedict and Hildegard of Bingen), and contemplated the talk I would give that morning. My first topic of the day was 'O Oriens' – 'O Dayspring' – the wonderful prayer for Christ to come as light, which is set for prayer on the true solstice, 21 December. I should have been revising the talk, but instead I composed this sonnet. I was, of course, conscious of Donne's 'Nocturnal upon St Lucy's Day', and felt I wanted to respond: to reply to that harrowing excursion into darkness with my own 'diurnal' upon St Lucy's day, cherishing every scrap of light and watching, in the final couplet, for the advent of the Dayspring from on high.

14 DECEMBER

Autumn *David Baird*

Was certainly not winter, scholars say,
When holy habitation broke the chill
Of hearth-felt separation, icy still,
The love of life in man that Christmas day.
Was autumn, rather, if seasons speak true;
When green retreats from sight's still ling'ring gaze,
And creeping cold numbs sense in sundry ways,
While settling silence speaks of solitude.
Hope happens when conditions are as these;
Comes finally lock-armed with death and sin,
When deep'ning dark demands its full display.
Then fallen nature driven to her knees
Flames russet, auburn, orange fierce from within,
And bush burns brighter for the growing grey.

As we saw from yesterday's poem, one motif that must run
through any collection of Advent poetry, gathered in and drawing
from the literature of northern Europe, is a sense of season. This
is very much the concern of the next two poems. The tradition
of holding the Feast of the Nativity on 25 December certainly
stretches back as far as AD 400, possibly earlier. And there are
many symbolically resonant reasons for celebrating the coming
of 'the true light' who enlightens all that come into the world
(John 1.9) into human flesh in this dark season. But symbolism is
concerned with one kind of truth, and historical source criticism
with another. Usually the two don't meet. David Baird, who holds

degrees in philosophy and theology from Wheaton College and Oxford University and works in the field of theology and the arts at St Andrew's, represents a rising generation of Christian writers and thinkers who are trying to hold the worlds of scholarship and poetry, of history and mythology, of reason and imagination, together in a fruitful conversation. So this playful poem, 'Autumn', first published in *Christendom Review* in 2014, begins by taking cognizance of the fact that the December celebration may have more to do with baptizing the Saturnalian winter festivals and allowing some continuity for newly converted pagans than with any firm knowledge of the date of Jesus' birth. Scholars have speculated about the date of Jesus' birth from the earliest times, as Baird himself has remarked, citing a letter of the Church Father Clement of Alexandria:

> There are those who have determined not only the year of our Lord's birth, but also the day; and they say that it took place in the 28th year of Augustus, and in the 25th day of [the Egyptian month] Pachon [May 20 in our calendar].

In fact, his point of departure in this poem is further recent scholarly speculation that it may have been in autumn. Even though the poem opens by formally rejecting the winter date, Baird nevertheless avails himself of the symbolism of hearth on the one hand and ice on the other, even as he dismisses it:

> Was certainly not winter, scholars say,
> When holy habitation broke the chill
> Of hearth-felt separation, icy still,
> The love of life in man that Christmas day.

There are some fine wordplays at work here. The word made flesh makes his 'holy habitation' among us even as the poem challenges the 'holy habit' of keeping a winter Christmas. Likewise, what might be 'heartfelt sympathy' becomes 'hearth-felt separation', sharing its line with 'icy still'. To be around the hearth-fire is precisely to be separated from the cold. But it is the 'chill' of our separation from the Holy that the Christ-child has come to break. The next four lines introduce the alternative of autumn, with its sense of decay and retreat.

Was autumn, rather, if seasons speak true;
When green retreats from sight's still ling'ring gaze,
And creeping cold numbs sense in sundry ways,
While settling silence speaks of solitude.

Then Baird keeps the Petrarchan tradition of the *volta*, the significant turn that begins the sestet, the last six lines of the sonnet. These start with the strong and affirmative alliteration, 'Hope happens'. It is as though he is saying: suppose I give scholarship its due, lose my holy habits, and start thinking of the Incarnation in autumn, even then the seasons and the symbols will be on my side; there is no season in which nature will not teach me something of the meaning of Christ's coming. Let us look more closely at what he says.

Hope happens when conditions are as these;
Comes finally lock-armed with death and sin,
When deep'ning dark demands its full display.

The idea of hope 'lock-armed with death and sin' is both striking and, I think, deliberately ambiguous. Are they 'lock-armed' in the sense that they are locked in mortal combat, with a possible residual play on the word 'armed'? Are they 'lock-armed' in the sense of Jacob and his wrestling angel, that one will not let the other go until some healing happens? Hope, even in the deepening dark, will not abandon death and sin. The breaking of the chill, and the making of a holy habitation, mean that experiences of sin and death need not be hopeless. Then, in the final three lines, comes a beautiful and redemptive turn that depends precisely on the autumnal season:

Then fallen nature driven to her knees
Flames russet, auburn, orange fierce from within,
And bush burns brighter for the growing grey.

Though this 'mid-Atlantic poet' has chosen to call his poem by the English name 'Autumn', he can still summon American energies in his choice of the word 'fallen'. The fall allows even 'fallen nature' to flame for a moment with beauty. And that flaming, even in the dark time, when things are growing grey, summons, as did Scott Cairns' 'Annunciation', the great archetype of Incarnation: the burning bush, in whose leaves the Divine shines out without consuming the natural, and whose roots make our ground holy.

15 DECEMBER

Christmas and Common Birth *Anne Ridler*

Christmas declares the glory of the flesh:
And therefore a European might wish
To celebrate it not at midwinter but in spring,
When physical life is strong,
When the consent to live is forced even on the young,
Juice is in the soil, the leaf, the vein,
Sugar flows to movement in limbs and brain.
Also before a birth, nourishing the child
We turn again to the earth
With unusual longing – to what is rich, wild,
Substantial: scents that have been stored and strengthened
In apple lofts, the underwash of woods, and in barns;
Drawn through the lengthened root; pungent in cones
(While the fir wood stands waiting; the beech wood aspiring,
Each in a different silence), and breaking out in spring
With scent sight sound indivisible in song.

Yet if you think again
It is good that Christmas comes at the dark dream of the year
That might wish to sleep ever.
For birth is awaking, birth is effort and pain;
And now at midwinter are the hints, inklings
(Sodden primrose, honeysuckle greening)
That sleep must be broken.
To bear new life or learn to live is an exacting joy:
The whole self must waken; you cannot predict the way

It will happen, or master the responses beforehand.
For any birth makes an inconvenient demand;
Like all holy things
It is frequently a nuisance, and its needs never end;
Freedom it brings: We should welcome release
From its long merciless rehearsal of peace.

So Christ comes
At the iron senseless time, comes
To force the glory into frozen veins:
His warmth wakes
Green life glazed in the pool, wakes
All calm and crystal trance with the living pains.

And each year
In seasonal growth is good – year
That lacking love is a stale story at best
By God's birth
Our common birth is holy; birth
Is all at Christmas time and wholly blest.

Born in 1912, Anne Ridler lived through all the rest of the long, difficult twentieth century, feeling the pulse of her times but never losing the sense of transcendence or the way eternal glory could suddenly rouse us and blaze through the ordinary. A friend of T. S. Eliot and Charles Williams, she joined with them in ensuring that threads of the sacred and of Christian witness were woven into the cloth of modernism. Drawn from her collection *The Nine Bright Shiners* (1943), 'Christmas and Common Birth' is one of a cluster of poems around the theme of childbirth, clearly written as she was having children herself, and it is that first-hand experience of expecting and delivering a baby that gives this poem its truth and authority. Other titles in that cluster include 'For a Child Expected' and 'For a Christening'.

Like yesterday's 'Autumn', this poem plays with the seasons, meditating on the way the outer season of the world may or may not reflect the inner season of the heart. After the wonderful declamatory opening line, 'Christmas declares the glory of the flesh', comes an evocation of what might be, in Eliot's phrase, a 'midwinter spring', but then she turns in the second stanza to a beautiful reflection on what it means to have Christmas come in winter, 'at the dark dream of the year'. This metaphor leads to a rich meditation on sleep and waking, and on how the coming of Christ rouses us from spiritual sleepiness into a new waking, or wakefulness, all figured in the coming of the child:

> For birth is awaking, birth is effort and pain;
> And now at midwinter are the hints, inklings
> (Sodden primrose, honeysuckle greening)
> That sleep must be broken.

Here all wakefulness is itself a kind of spring. But this image is not sentimentalized or over-poeticized. This is the poem of a mother who knows only too well that

> you cannot predict the way
> It will happen, or master the responses beforehand.
> For any birth makes an inconvenient demand;
> Like all holy things
> It is frequently a nuisance, and its needs never end;

And that is why

> To bear new life or learn to live is an exacting joy:
> The whole self must waken;

The paradox of the 'exacting joy' is at the heart of the poem. Labour is difficult and all babies make demands, but even in that pain and exaction there is utter joy and new creation. After the two long-line stanzas comes a lovely little pendant two-verse lyric (this technique of alternating forms is something she may have learned from Eliot, who was writing the *Four Quartets* at this time; and it must be a conscious imitation of the two-poem structure of Milton's 'Ode on the Morning of Christ's Nativity' – see

Christmas Day). Here the paradox of Life coming in midwinter, light in darkness, glory through flesh, transformation through 'living pains', is given a memorable musical expression, the initial short lines unfolding and expanding out to living fullness:

> His warmth wakes
> Green life glazed in the pool, wakes
> All calm and crystal trance with the living pains.

In the last line the whole poem turns back to its beginning and we realize that the 'glory of the flesh' declared at Christmas is not simply the glory of the holy flesh of the Christ-child, or some special Christmas-card glow around only the holy family; it is really the glory given by the Incarnation to all flesh and at every birth:

> By God's birth
> Our common birth is holy; birth
> Is all at Christmas time and wholly blest.

16 DECEMBER

Advent Good Wishes *David Grieve*

Give you joy, wolf,
when Messiah makes you meek
and turns your roar into a cry that
justice has been done for the poor.

Give you joy, lamb,
when Messiah saves you from jeopardy
and all fear is overwhelmed
by his converting grace.

Give you joy, wolf and lamb together,
as Messiah brings worldwide peace and,
side by side, you shelter
under Jesse's spreading shoot.

How early do you start to send out Christmas cards? If, like many, you find that mid-Advent brings panic about not having sent good wishes for a season that is not yet with us, then perhaps David Grieve's 'Advent Good Wishes' is a salutary antidote. Let's forget the Christmas cards for a moment and share Advent good wishes with our fellow creatures! A priest-poet living in the Diocese of Durham and chaplain at the Cathedral there, Grieve offers us a meditation on Isaiah 11.6–9:

The wolf shall live with the lamb,
the leopard shall lie down with the kid,
the calf and the lion and the fatling together,

and a little child shall lead them.
The cow and the bear shall graze,
their young shall lie down together;
and the lion shall eat straw like the ox.
The nursing child shall play over the hole of the asp,
and the weaned child shall put its hand on the adder's den.
They will not hurt or destroy
on all my holy mountain;
for the earth will be full of the knowledge of the LORD
as the waters cover the sea.

But here the poet has restored a freshness and wonder to an oft-quoted prophecy by changing it from the third to the second person. We are not observing the wolf and the lamb of some distant future, but with an almost Franciscan inflection we are invited to address the wolf and the lamb now, so that they too can share our Advent hope. The simple language of this poem takes us gently from the outward and visible signs to the inward and spiritual truth of this prophecy in those three key words: justice, peace and grace.

Our Advent focus is lifted beyond Christmas, far beyond the brief nine days before festivities commence, to glimpse in mystery and beauty the great festivity, the kingdom glory to which, in Isaiah's prophecy and by Christ's death and resurrection, all creation moves. Isaiah's vision is like a positive picture intuited from the exposed 'negative' of our shadowed and fallen experience. We live in a world of predator and prey, tragedy and accident, a world where by mishap or by deliberate evil 'they' always seem to 'hurt and destroy'. And yet every time these 'normal' and 'natural' tragedies occur we are outraged, and rightly so. We feel deeply that this is not 'normal', not how things are meant to be. Even if we have never read the text, we all share Isaiah's vision of restored peace on the holy mountain; we yearn for an unveiling and revelation of glory that will end the shadows and the bloodshed. That too is an essential element of our Advent hope, bound to the story of Christmas because, in the end, the little child who will lead them is the one born in Bethlehem.

17 DECEMBER

O Sapientia

O Sapientia, quae ex ore Altissimi prodiisti,
attingens a fine usque ad finem,
fortiter suaviterque disponens omnia:
veni ad docendum nos viam prudentiae.

O Wisdom, coming forth from the mouth of the Most High,
reaching from one end to the other mightily,
and sweetly ordering all things:
Come and teach us the way of prudence.

O Sapientia *Malcolm Guite*

I cannot think unless I have been thought,
Nor can I speak unless I have been spoken.
I cannot teach except as I am taught,
Or break the bread except as I am broken.
O Mind behind the mind through which I seek,
O Light within the light by which I see,
O Word beneath the words with which I speak,
O founding, unfound Wisdom, finding me,
O sounding Song whose depth is sounding me,
O Memory of time, reminding me,
My Ground of Being, always grounding me,
My Maker's Bounding Line, defining me,
  Come, hidden Wisdom, come with all you bring,
  Come to me now, disguised as everything.

This is the first sonnet in a sequence of seven I have written in response to the seven Advent prayers known as the 'O Antiphons'. In its first centuries the Church developed a custom of praying seven great prayers, calling afresh on Christ to come, addressing him by the mysterious titles found in the Old Testament, particularly in Isaiah: 'O Wisdom!' 'O Root!' 'O Key!' 'O Light!' 'O Emmanuel!'

These prayers were said 'antiphonally', as the name suggests, either side of the Magnificat at Vespers from 17 to 23 December (although in some places they begin a day earlier, on 16 December). Each antiphon begins with the invocation 'O' and then calls on Christ, although never by name. The mysterious titles and emblems given him from the pages of the Old Testament touch on our deepest needs and intuitions; then each antiphon prays the great Advent verb, *Veni*, 'Come!'

There is, I think, both wisdom and humility in this strange abstention from the name of Christ in a Christian prayer. Of course, these prayers were composed AD, perhaps around the seventh century, but in another sense, Advent itself is always BC! The whole purpose of Advent is to be for a moment fully and consciously Before Christ. In that place of darkness and waiting, we look for his coming and do not presume too much that we already know or have it. Whoever compiled these prayers was able, imaginatively, to write 'BC', perhaps saying to themselves: 'If I hadn't heard of Christ, and didn't know the name of Jesus, I would still long for a saviour. I would still need someone to come. Who would I need? I would need a gift of Wisdom, I would need a Light, a King, a Root, a Key, a Flame.' And poring over the pages of the Old Testament, they would find all these things promised in the coming of Christ. By calling on Christ using each of these seven several gifts and prophecies we learn afresh the meaning of a perhaps too familiar name. It might be a good Advent exercise, and paradoxically an aid to sharing the faith, if for a season we didn't rush in our conversation to refer to the known name, the predigested knowledge, the formulae of our faith, but waited alongside our non-Christian neighbours, who are, of course, living 'BC'. We should perhaps count ourselves among the people who walk in darkness but look for a marvellous light. In making these seven sonnets in response to the antiphons, I have tried to do that, looking at both my own deepest needs and our common needs, to inhabit some of the darkness that waits for a light.

The first antiphon is 'O Sapientia', 'O Wisdom'. It draws on two passages from the Apocrypha praising wisdom. And it is clear from these passages that the wisdom described in this antiphon is not the private capacity of an individually wise person or the accumulated prudence of a human 'wisdom tradition'; it is a primal, almost pre-existent, quality of order and beauty out of which all things spring. Though they speak of wisdom in the feminine, a divine being delighting before God and with him ordering the cosmos, it is clear that for the writer of this antiphon, Sapientia is part of what John means by the Logos, 'the Word [who] was with God' (John 1.1), the coming Christ. In Wisdom of Solomon 8.1 (AV), we read: 'Wisdom reacheth from one end to another mightily: and sweetly doth she order all things.' And then in Ecclesiasticus, the beautiful extended passage:

> Wisdom shall praise herself, and shall glory in the midst of her
> people.
> In the congregation of the most High shall she open her mouth,
> and triumph before his power.
> I came out of the mouth of the most High, and covered the
> earth as a cloud.
> I dwelt in high places, and my throne is in a cloudy pillar.
> I alone compassed the circuit of heaven, and walked in the
> bottom of the deep.
> In the waves of the sea and in all the earth, and in every people
> and nation, I got a possession.
> With all these I sought rest: and in whose inheritance shall I
> abide?
> So the Creator of all things gave me a commandment, and he
> that made me caused my tabernacle to rest, and said, Let thy
> dwelling be in Jacob, and thine inheritance in Israel.

He created me from the beginning before the world, and I shall
never fail.
(Ecclesiasticus 24.1–9, AV)

It is this Wisdom we address, and for whose advent we pray when
we look for the coming of Christ.

In my sonnet I wanted to convey this sense of the underlying
and underpinning order of things, the 'Mind behind the mind
through which I seek ... Light within the light by which I see'.
Writing the poem led me in the end to a strange paradox. The
psalmist is taunted by the question, 'Where is now your God?'
And it's a question that some more militant 'scientific' atheists
of our own day still use to taunt Christians. And in one sense we
cannot directly point to God because *Sapientia*, this underlying
coherence and beauty, is not to be found anywhere as an item in
the cosmos; it is not a single being, but the ground of being itself
– not a single beauty but the source of all beauty. And yet, for the
very same reason, there is a real sense in which we can point to
everything, 'from one end to the other' of the cosmos, and say,
'There, can't you see?' For wisdom is both hidden and gloriously
apparent.

Come, hidden Wisdom, come with all you bring,
Come to me now, disguised as everything.

18 DECEMBER

O Adonai

O Adonai, et Dux domus Israel,
qui Moysi in igne flammae rubi apparuisti,
et ei in Sina legem dedisti:
veni ad redimendum nos in brachio extento.

O Adonai, and leader of the House of Israel,
who appeared to Moses in the fire of the burning bush
and gave him the law on Sinai:
Come and redeem us with an outstretched arm.

O Adonai *Malcolm Guite*

Unsayable, you chose to speak one tongue,
Unseeable, you gave yourself away,
The Adonai, the Tetragramaton
Grew by a wayside in the light of day.
O you who dared to be a tribal God,
To own a language, people and a place,
Who chose to be exploited and betrayed,
If so you might be met with face to face,
Come to us here, who would not find you there,
Who chose to know the skin and not the pith,
Who heard no more than thunder in the air,
Who marked the mere events and not the myth.
Touch the bare branches of our unbelief
And blaze again like fire in every leaf.

Today we turn to the second of these antiphons, 'O Adonai'. As a prayer this antiphon is drawing together two different parts of the Exodus story:

> There the angel of the LORD appeared to him in a flame of fire out of a bush; and he looked, and the bush was blazing, yet it was not consumed. (Exodus 3.2)

> The LORD said to Moses, 'Come up to me on the mountain, and wait there; and I will give you the tablets of stone, with the law and the commandment, which I have written for their instruction'. (Exodus 24.12)

'O Adonai' touches on the ancient title of God himself (*Adonai* meaning 'Lord') used in the Old Testament, because his sacred name, the four letters known as the 'tetragrammaton', could not be uttered by mere human beings without blasphemy. But the Advent hope – indeed, the Advent miracle – was that this unknowable, un-namable, utterly holy Lord chose out of his own free will and out of love for us to become known: to bear a name and meet us where we are. The antiphon prayer reflects on the mysterious and awesome manifestations of God to Moses on the mountain in the burning bush. For early Christians, this bush, full of the fire of God's presence, yet still itself and unconsumed, was a sign of the Lord Christ who would come, who would be fully God and yet also fully human. We saw earlier, in Scott Cairns' poem 'Annunciation' and again in David Baird's 'Autumn', how the burning bush somehow embodies and bears forth the coming miracle of Christmas. Some of these themes are woven into the sonnet, which also faces head on what has been called the scandal of particularity. 'O Sapientia', taken by itself, might leave us free to agree with one another vaguely on an equally vague and amorphous religion in which something undoubtedly holy was generally everywhere, but no one need make any particular claims or have any awkward personal encounters: a high religion for the high-minded, but no earthly use. By contrast, the core of the Christian faith, and indeed of Judaism before it, concerns a

God who meets particular people in particular places, and from one small encounter builds a nation and changes everything. To believe in such a God is to make a claim for the importance of actual encounter, real occurrence, and ultimately to believe that audacious mystery with which we opened this poetic sequence in Donne's 'Annunciation': that immensity was 'cloister'd in thy dear womb'. When I became a Christian as an undergraduate I remember an anthropology student sneering at me, saying, 'The God of the Old Testament is just a tribal god.' In this sonnet, I finally answer back and say, 'Yes, it's just as well he dared to be, dared to come out of the invulnerable realm of ideas and into the bloody theatre of history, that he might change and redeem it from within.'

19 DECEMBER

O Radix

O Radix Jesse, qui stas in signum populorum,
super quem continebunt reges os suum,
quem Gentes deprecabuntur:
veni ad liberandum nos, jam noli tardare.

O Root of Jesse, standing as a sign among the peoples;
before you kings will shut their mouths,
to you the nations will make their prayer:
Come and deliver us, and delay no longer.

O Radix *Malcolm Guite*

All of us sprung from one deep-hidden seed,
Rose from a root invisible to all.
We knew the virtues once of every weed,
But, severed from the roots of ritual,
We surf the surface of a wide-screen world
And find no virtue in the virtual.
We shrivel on the edges of a wood
Whose heart we once inhabited in love,
Now we have need of you, forgotten Root,
The stock and stem of every living thing
Whom once we worshipped in the sacred grove,
For now is winter, now is withering
Unless we let you root us deep within,
Under the ground of being, graft us in.

The third Advent Antiphon, 'O Radix', is a prayer that calls on Christ as the Root, an image I find particularly compelling and helpful. The antiphon refers to the image of the 'tree of Jesse', the family tree that leads to David and ultimately to Christ as the 'Son of David': 'On that day the root of Jesse shall stand as a signal to the peoples; the nations shall inquire of him, and his dwellings shall be glorious' (Isaiah 11.10). But for me the title 'Radix' goes deeper, as a good root should, deep down into the ground of our being, the good soil of creation. God in Christ is, I believe, the root of all goodness, wherever it is found and in whatsoever culture, or with whatever names it fruits and flowers. A sound tree cannot bear bad fruit, said Christ, who also said, 'I am the vine, you are the branches' (John 15.5).

It may be worth opening out some details of the sonnet. In the third and sixth lines, I make some play with the word 'virtue'. This interesting word can still be used in two distinct ways, showing something of its root meaning. We probably think first of virtue in purely ethical terms: the four cardinal virtues (prudence, justice, temperance and fortitude) and the three theological virtues (hope, faith and charity). We may strive to be virtuous or admire the virtue of others. Indeed, in the field of ethics the idea of virtue has made a recent and helpful return, described in Alasdair Mac-Intyre's groundbreaking book *After Virtue* (1981). For a while, 'situation ethics', and various reductive forms of behaviourism, were in danger of reducing people to no more than bundles of manipulable complexes and responses, a view in which there could be no virtue or vice at all, indeed no real personhood or decision-making. The return to virtue ethics has acknowledged a sense of rootedness, coherence, responsibility: the deliberate cultivation and owning of chosen behaviours understood once more as intrinsically better, more 'virtuous', than others. This new strengthening of ethical discourse leads on to the other sense of the word virtue, and indeed which was its original sense: 'intrinsic strength or power'. So the medieval herbalists would say that a particular herb has 'healing virtue', meaning intrinsic goodness. Virtue in this sense is not just an acquired behaviour, but a re-rooting in the true virtues, the intrinsic qualities by virtue of which we are human. For this reason, as I suggest in lines five and six, it is particularly ironic that we have chosen the word 'virtual' to describe the apparently amoral and essentially unreal free-play of cyberspace, where people can be constantly tempted to explore and make a display of their vices. In his poem 'Afternoons', Philip Larkin has an extraordinary line about the lives of people in post-war England:

Something is pushing them
To the side of their own lives.

I think I had this line in mind, and it seems truer now than when Larkin wrote it: there is a link between our rootlessness and our uncentred edginess. All these things are set out in the octet of my sonnet. The poem then turns with the sestet, beginning with the word 'Now', calling on Christ the Root to 'graft us in', language I have borrowed from Paul's letter to the Romans.

20 DECEMBER

O Clavis

O Clavis David, et sceptrum domus Israel;
qui aperis, et nemo claudit;
claudis, et nemo aperit:
veni, et educ vinctum de domo carceris,
sedentem in tenebris, et umbra mortis.

O Key of David and sceptre of the House of Israel;
you open and no one can shut;
you shut and no one can open:
Come and lead the prisoners from the prison house,
those who dwell in darkness and the shadow of death.

O Clavis *Malcolm Guite*

Even in the darkness where I sit
And huddle in the midst of misery
I can remember freedom, but forget
That every lock must answer to a key,
That each dark clasp, sharp and intricate,
Must find a counter-clasp to meet its guard,
Particular, exact and intimate,
The clutch and catch that meshes with its ward.

I cry out for the key I threw away
That turned and over turned with certain touch

And with the lovely lifting of a latch
Opened my darkness to the light of day.
O come again, come quickly, set me free
Cut to the quick to fit, the master key.

The compiler of this antiphon is drawing together two different but wonderfully complementary passages of Isaiah:

I will place on his shoulder the key of the house of David; he shall open, and no one shall shut; and he shall shut, and no one shall open. (Isaiah 22.22)

to open the eyes that are blind, to bring out the prisoners from the dungeon, from the prison those who sit in darkness. (Isaiah 42.7)

Of all the mystic titles of Christ, 'O Clavis', 'O Key', is the one that connects most closely with our 'secular' psychology. We speak of the need on the one hand for 'closure' and on the other for 'unlocking', 'opening' or 'liberation'. The same ideas are there in the lines from 'O come, O come, Emmanuel', drawn from this antiphon, which could easily be part of anybody's work in good therapy:

Make safe the way that leads on high,
and close the path to misery.

I see this antiphon, and the sonnet I wrote in response to it, as the 'before' picture that precedes the beautiful fifth antiphon, 'O Oriens', about Christ as the Dayspring. In this sonnet I found that I had at last written something clear about my own experience of depression. I hope that others who have been in that darkness will find it helpful.

As I contemplated the idea of Christ as a Key, two distinct memories came to me. One was of an enlightening passage from G. K. Chesterton's book *Orthodoxy*, in which he writes not directly about Christ but about the whole complex Christian Creed as *necessarily* complex, and strangely shaped because it has to fit the complex world we find ourselves in. Here's how Chesterton puts it:

> When once one believes in a creed, one is proud of its complexity, as scientists are proud of the complexity of science. It shows how rich it is in discoveries. If it is right at all, it is a compliment to say that it's elaborately right. A stick might fit a hole or a stone a hollow by accident. But a key and a lock are both complex. And if a key fits a lock, you know it is the right key. (Chapter 6, 'The Paradoxes of Christianity', p. 27)

The other, deeper and older memory was of being taken by my mother as a child to see a key being cut; not a little Yale one, but a big, old-fashioned, complex one. I remember the locksmith clamping the blank in the vice beside the key to which it would conform, and then the noise and violence of what followed, the high-pitched scream and whine of the metal cutter – in Seamus Heaney's words, 'the unpredictable fantail of sparks' – and the miracle of the finished thing, still cooling in the hand. Chesterton applied the image of the key to the Creed, but the antiphon applies it to Christ himself. Suddenly I came to see his Passion, the hammering blows he received, the searching wounds, as somehow the cutting that makes Christ a key that finally fits, unlocks, opens and heals our woundedness.

21 DECEMBER

O Oriens

O Oriens,
splendor lucis aeternae, et sol justitiae:
veni, et illumina sedentes in tenebris, et umbra mortis

O Dayspring,
splendour of light eternal and sun of righteousness:
Come and enlighten those who dwell in darkness and the
shadow of death.

O Oriens *Malcolm Guite*

E vidi lume in forme de riviera – Paradiso XXX, 61

First light and then first lines along the east
To touch and brush a sheen of light on water
As though behind the sky itself they traced

The shift and shimmer of another river
Flowing unbidden from its hidden source;
The Day-Spring, the eternal Prima Vera.

Blake saw it too. Dante and Beatrice
Are bathing in it now, away upstream ...
So every trace of light begins a grace

In me, a beckoning. The smallest gleam
Is somehow a beginning and a calling:
'Sleeper awake, the darkness was a dream

For you will see the Dayspring at your waking,
Beyond your long last line the dawn is breaking.'

But for you who revere my name the sun of righteousness shall
rise, with healing in its wings. You shall go out leaping like
calves from the stall. (Malachi 4.2)

Today brings us to the fifth great 'O Antiphon', which calls on
Christ as the *Oriens*, the Morning Star, the Dayspring, develop-
ing an image in Malachi. This antiphon comes as an answer to
the sense of darkness and captivity in the fourth Antiphon, 'O
Clavis'. I find the idea of Christ as a rising light in the east very
moving, for he is Alpha, the 'Beginning'. It is most appropriate
that this particular antiphon should be set on 21 December, the
winter solstice, for this is, in John Donne's phrase, 'the year's mid-
night' (see 13 December). On the shortest, darkest day of the year
the Church remembers and looks forward to the coming of 'the
light who has risen with healing in his wings'. Indeed, the title,
'O Oriens', offers a profound insight into the 'orientation' of the
spiritual life, and also the physical orientation of church build-
ings. It is a traditional poetic metaphor, to the point of being a
cliché, to think of the early morning and first light in the east as
analogous to the beginning of our lives, our childhood and youth,
of the noon as representing our years of full vigour and strength,
and the declining of the sun as representing our waning years.
This is why we have to endure such dreadful names of retirement
and nursing homes as Sunset View.

Chronologically, we may journey from the east to the west, but
spiritually the reverse is the case. Our churches face east, but the
font, which we might associate with birth and babyhood, is by
the west door; it is there, even in our infancy, that we deal with
our dying. We are baptized into that sunset and declination, made

one with Christ in his death, so that we might also be one with him in his resurrection. Thereafter, we move eastwards, towards that rising and beginning, that eternal Sabbath, the first day of the week, our sunrise. 'Even though our outer nature is wasting away, our inner nature is being renewed day by day' (2 Corinthians 4.16). 'Our salvation is nearer to us now than when we became believers' (Romans 13.11). C. S. Lewis expressed this perfectly in mythopoeic form in *The Voyage of the Dawn Treader*, the best of his Narnia books; he takes the pagan classical idea of the magical journey to the blessed isles, which in Homer and Virgil and the Voyages of Brendan are all in the west, and reorients it so that we sail eastwards towards sunrise, until, in an image borrowed from Dante, even the water becomes drinkable light. However much our *bios*, 'life of the flesh', may be headed quietly towards a retirement at Sunset View, this antiphon reminds us that in our true *zoe*, 'spiritual life', we are all 'dawn-treaders'. The translation giving 'Dayspring' for *Oriens* I especially love, because 'Dayspring' suggests at one and the same time both light and water: two primal goods in life that are particularly appealing in combination, especially light reflected on water.

It may be helpful to open out a little more of what I was drawing on when writing this sonnet. Certainly, *The Voyage of the Dawn Treader* was in my mind, but so too was one of Lewis' sources for that book, Dante's 'Paradiso'. The epigraph to my poem, '*E vidi lume in forme de riviera*', translates as 'And I saw light in the form of a river'. Dante is making direct reference to the description of the river of life in the book of Revelation, as well perhaps as to his reading of Virgil and his personal memories of the lost paradise of Florence and the light on the Arno. When Dante first meets Virgil at the beginning of *The Divine Comedy*, he cries out in delight:

you are that Virgil,
whose words flow wide, a river running full?
You are the light and glory of all poets.
('Inferno', lines 80–2)

As I said in my commentary on this passage in *The Word in the Wilderness*:

> Those two images, the flowing river and the glory of light, are the key elements in the 'Paradiso', where indeed, having left Virgil behind, Dante says, 'I saw light as a flowing river'. It may be that hidden in the poets and writers we love best is a vital clue about the heaven we are aiming for; that we should stay with and return often and with confidence to those lines and images that have most inspired us, even from our childhood.

In this sonnet I have taken a leaf out of Dante's book, by fusing my own memories of favourite poets, including Dante, with personal memories of light and water in order to incarnate and body forth what these paradisal images mean. I wrote this poem at dawn, sitting in the cockpit of a little boat called 'Dayspring', watching the sunrise over the River Orwell on the east coast of England, recovering from a long period of darkness. There seemed to me to be something magical in the very word 'Dayspring', combining as it does images of light and water. If I may mention it, there is also a personal *pietas* towards my great-grandfather, who designed, built and named a ship 'Dayspring', as a gift to Scottish missionaries: that the 'Dayspring' in every sense might visit people with the message of salvation. A spring is both a point of renewal and a source, and I believe that the Christian life is a reorientation, a turning eastwards and upstream, towards the source of life and light that is always flowing towards us. And so I imagine all the saints and the poets who have formed me – Dante and Blake – somehow ahead of me in that rising light, playing in the river upstream.

22 DECEMBER

O Rex Gentium

O Rex Gentium, et desideratus earum,
lapisque angularis, qui facis utraque unum:
veni, et salva hominem,
quem de limo formasti.

O King of the nations, and their desire,
the cornerstone making both one:
Come and save the human race,
which you fashioned from clay.

O Rex Gentium *Malcolm Guite*

O King of our desire whom we despise,
King of the nations never on the throne,
Unfound foundation, cast-off cornerstone,
Rejected joiner, making many one,
You have no form or beauty for our eyes,
A King who comes to give away his crown,
A King within our rags of flesh and bone.
We pierce the flesh that pierces our disguise,
For we ourselves are found in you alone.
Come to us now and find in us your throne,
O King within the child within the clay,
O hidden King who shapes us in the play
Of all creation. Shape us for the day
Your coming Kingdom comes into its own.

Therefore thus says the Lord GOD, See, I am laying in Zion for a foundation stone, a tested stone, a precious cornerstone, a sure foundation: 'One who trusts will not panic.' (Isaiah 28.16)

For he is our peace; in his flesh he has made both groups into one and has broken down the dividing wall, that is, the hostility between us. (Ephesians 2.14)

Today we read the sixth great 'O Antiphon', 'O Rex Gentium'. This antiphon calls on Christ as King, yet also calls him the cornerstone and pictures him getting his hands dirty and shaping us with clay: a wonderfully incongruous combination!

In the first four lines of the sonnet I have tried to compress and emphasize the paradoxes that are involved in calling this poor carpenter our King, rather as Donne does with the paradoxes of the Annunciation. The antiphon boldly proclaims Christ as 'the desire of all nations' (Haggai 2.7, AV). But the truth is that this 'desire of nations' was in fact rejected by his own nation, to whom he came, and crucified by the power of an empire that comprised most of the other known nations. If there is something deep within us all that does indeed desire Christ, we must also be aware of and confess those forces within us and within our culture that also despise and reject him.

He is hailed as *Rex Gentium*, King of the nations, but in this life, and in the history of the world, he has never been crowned, except with thorns. He is 'a precious cornerstone, a sure foundation' (Isaiah 28.16), but, as Peter observed when quoting that line of Isaiah in his epistle, the cornerstone had become 'a stone that makes them stumble, and a rock that makes them fall' (1 Peter 2.8). He would have learned from Joseph in his trade as a carpenter the art of making sure joints and connections, of dovetailing disparate pieces of wood together to make a firm structure, as indeed he does for us in the Church. I remember coming across a wayside pulpit once that simply read: 'Carpenter seeks joiners'! But for most people in our culture he is still, as I observe in this sonnet, a 'rejected joiner'.

Indeed, to call the carpenter of Nazareth a king is radically to subvert, and to reimagine, the meaning of kingship. Christ himself makes this explicit for us on Maundy Thursday, when he takes the bowl and the towel and washes the feet of his disciples, declaring 'I am among you as one who serves' (Luke 22.27). In the idea of the rejected joiner, the itinerant carpenter who is in truth a hidden king, we find a reference to one of the deepest motifs of our own folklore and mythology: from King Lear, out on the heath, in the storm, willingly so to feel alongside poor Tom O'Bedlam the worst of life, and calling on other kings to do the same,

> take physic, pomp,
> expose thyself to feel what wretches feel ...

through to the story of Henry V, moving in disguise among the campfires of his own soldiers; to its most recent and powerful iteration is the figure of Strider in *The Lord of the Rings*, the ragged ranger who walks with the Fellowship on the long road, before they eventually discover that he is their true king. Perhaps we love these stories of the hidden king because we realize that that is how God has come to us. But today's antiphon has one more paradoxical turn,

> Come and save the human race,
> which you fashioned from clay.

This petition takes us to that extraordinary moment in Genesis (2.7) when the Lord God formed the human being out of the dust of the ground. In the context of the Genesis narrative this verse forms a startling contrast with the opening cosmic passage in which an all-powerful and divine being calls the universe into existence with a mere word, 'let there be light'. In this 'second narrative', as it is sometimes called, the compiler of Genesis presents us with something much more tactile, human and hands-on: the artist forming the model in clay, perhaps even the child playing with the earth. I have drawn on both these ideas in the final quatrain of my poem, suggesting that the childlike in God, the child in the midst to whom the kingdom of heaven belongs, is perhaps there, even 'in the beginning', in our making. When we in turn are making and shaping ourselves and our world, there within us is also something of this same divine child. I don't think this making and shaping is over. We are still being formed by the divine hands, from the dust of the ground. I remember being at a Christian music festival and wanting to rebuke the teenagers in the tent next to mine for having kept me up all night with their exuberance and music, but then one of them emerged from his tent wearing a T-shirt that read 'Be patient, God hasn't finished with me yet'. I took the rebuke, and was glad to know that God hasn't finished with me yet either. Indeed, as Advent calls us to look for the fruition of all things, for the coming of the kingdom that is both here and yet to come, it is good to know that not only we ourselves, but our whole world are clay in the potter's hands.[2]

---

2 There is a beautiful elaboration of this in Diana Glyers' excellent book *Clay in the Potter's Hands* (Lindale & Associates, 2011).

23 DECEMBER

O Emmanuel

O Emmanuel, Rex et legifer noster,
exspectatio Gentium, et Salvator earum:
veni ad salvandum nos, Domine, Deus noster.

O Emmanuel, our king and our lawgiver,
the hope of the nations and their Saviour:
Come and save us, O Lord our God.

O Emmanuel *Malcolm Guite*

O come, O come, and be our God-with-us
O long-sought With-ness for a world without,
O secret seed, O hidden spring of light.
Come to us Wisdom, come unspoken Name,
Come Root, and Key, and King, and holy Flame.
O quickened little wick so tightly curled,
Be folded with us into time and place,
Unfold for us the mystery of grace
And make a womb of all this wounded world.
O heart of heaven beating in the earth,
O tiny hope within our hopelessness
Come to be born, to bear us to our birth,
To touch a dying world with new-made hands
And make these rags of time our swaddling bands.

Therefore the Lord himself shall give you a sign. Behold, a virgin woman shall conceive and bear a son, and shall call his name Immanu-el. (Isaiah 7.14, AV)

So we come to the last of the seven great 'O Antiphons', sung either side of the Magnificat: 'O Emmanuel', 'O God with us'.

I sometimes think that Christianity is not so much a *propositional* religion as a *prepositional* religion: everything turns on the prepositions, the tiny little words that define and change relationships. So much of pagan religion was about God's aboveness, immortals over against mortals, eternity in contradistinction to time, about transcendence, disconnect and otherness. But Christianity brings these little words: *in*, 'Christ in you, the hope of glory' (Colossians 1.27); *for*, 'if God is for us, who is against us?' (Romans 8.31); *through*, 'we make our prayer to the Father through the Son and in the Spirit'; and most supremely in this Advent and Christmas time, *with*, 'God with us'. This little word 'with' is good news for a world without; so often without hope, without love, without meaning. In late Western modernity we have constructed an atomized, value-free, material model of reality in which our islanded selves are ultimately disconnected from one another. T. S. Eliot put his finger on it in the *Choruses from The Rock*:

When the Stranger says: 'What is the meaning of this city?
Do you huddle close together because you love each other?'
What will you answer? 'We all dwell together
To make money from each other'? or 'This is a community'?

Perhaps it is only when we grasp the fundamental gospel, the 'good news', that in our Emmanuel God is *with* us, that we can seriously begin to be *with* one another.

In this final sonnet of the sequence I look back across the other titles of Christ, but also look forward, beyond Christmas, to the new birth for humanity and for the whole cosmos that is promised in the birth of God in our midst. For the birth of Christ at Christmas is the sign of the other birth that Christ promises: the birth of the kingdom of God, and ourselves born anew within it. Indeed, he says of the pains of his Passion that they are the birth-pangs of his kingdom. 'When a woman is in labour, she has pain, because her hour has come. But when her child is born, she no longer remembers the anguish because of the joy of having brought a human being into the world' (John 16.21). This is what led me to use the phrase, 'And make a womb of all this wounded world'. In the Christmas story Christ is wrapped in swaddling bands. We only come to know the significance of that wrapping when we reach the parallel moment when he is wrapped in grave-clothes, for they are the swaddling bands of the new kingdom; these he unwraps and lays aside at the moment of his resurrection and our new birth. In the exultant conclusion of his beautiful love poem 'The Sun Rising', John Donne says, 'Love all alike no season knows nor clime nor hours days months which are the rags of time'. I took up and renewed this line in the conclusion of my sonnet, suggesting that time itself is the swaddling band/grave-cloth from which God's kingdom will release us.

This final antiphon, from which our lovely Advent hymn 'O come, O come, Emmanuel' takes its origin, reveals a secret message that is embedded subtly into the whole sequence. In each of these antiphons we have been calling on him to come to us, to come as Light, as Key, as King, as God-with-us. Now, standing on the brink of Christmas Eve, looking back at the illuminated capital letters for each of the seven titles of Christ, we would see an answer to our pleas:

O Emmanuel
O Rex
O Oriens
O Clavis
O Radix
O Adonai
O Sapientia

Ero cras: the Latin words meaning 'Tomorrow I will come!'

24 DECEMBER

Christmas Eve *Christina Rossetti*

Christmas hath darkness
Brighter than the blazing noon,
Christmas hath a chillness
Warmer than the heat of June,
Christmas hath a beauty
Lovelier than the world can show:
For Christmas bringeth Jesus,
Brought for us so low.

Earth, strike up your music,
Birds that sing and bells that ring;
Heaven hath answering music
For all Angels soon to sing:
Earth, put on your whitest
Bridal robe of spotless snow:
For Christmas bringeth Jesus,
Brought for us so low.

This deceptively simple and musical lyric by Christina Rossetti brings us to Christmas Eve. But for all its incantatory rhythm and lilting feel, this is not some shallow rhyme or the pious platitudes we encounter in many a Victorian hymn. Rather, it adumbrates the themes, and goes right to the heart of those paradoxes we have been contemplating throughout Advent: darkness and light, winter and spring, the meeting of heaven and earth; and, above all, the theme of kenosis, the self-emptying, the courteous descent of our loving God into human flesh. For many people in our consumer society the loud, brash, insistent, garish, glaring Christmas lights, the constant background muzak, the winking tinsel and trivial shininess of everything can become, ironically, very oppressive. And it's in that context that we can welcome the beautiful paradox with which this poem opens:

Christmas hath darkness
Brighter than the blazing noon

In a garish world, it is down in the darkness that we will find our light. Rossetti is drawing here both on the description of the light Paul encountered at his conversion: 'At midday, O king, I saw in the way a light from heaven, above the brightness of the sun, shining round about me and them which journeyed with me' (Acts 26.13, AV), and also remembering Milton's phrasing of God's brightness from *Paradise Lost*:

Drawn round about thee like a radiant Shrine,
Dark with excessive bright thy skirts appeer,
Yet dazle Heav'n.
(Book III, lines 379–81)

Once again, we have a poet who is embracing rather than resisting the dark and cold at this time of year. And there is something very moving in the simplicity and long reach of the repeating line – the 'burden' as it is technically called – at the end of each verse: 'Brought for us so low'. In one sense this is a direct reference to the Philippians kenosis passage, and to the Creed, 'He came down from heaven': the Incarnation is itself a coming down and being brought low. But surely this phrase reaches further. We know that the Incarnation is just the beginning of the divine descent, and that he will be brought low in the modern sense: low spirits, darkness, depression, the agony in the garden; and he will be brought low down through the grave and gate of death, and lower still, descending into hell. And all 'for us', for however low we fall, we will always find that still 'underneath are the everlasting arms' (Deuteronomy 33.27).

The second verse turns from the paradox of darkness and light to music as the medium for a meeting of heaven and earth, but again, Rossetti introduces an interesting reversal. It might seem usual to think of the heavenly music first, and then earth in some sense 'answering'. But Rossetti wants us to view the whole Incarnation as a kind of answer from heaven to earth. So she starts with the earthly music and looks for the answer of the heavenly angels:

Earth, strike up your music,
Birds that sing and bells that ring;
Heaven hath answering music
For all Angels soon to sing.

These words are perfect for Christmas Eve, as we tremble on the brink and in silence, waiting for the annunciation of that music. Throughout this verse, Christina Rossetti is drawing on Milton's 'Ode on the Morning of Christ's Nativity', which we read tomorrow. From that she takes the image of the ringing bells, though in Milton it is the crystal spheres of heaven that ring first. And she also draws the idea of the snow as a white robe worn by the earth. Though again, she does not simply echo it, but gives it a new meaning. Milton writes:

Only with speeches fair
She wooes the gentle air
To hide her guilty front with innocent snow;
And on her naked shame,
Pollute with sinful blame,
The saintly veil of maiden white to throw

In Milton's poem, the veil of white snow is there in some sense to hide shame and deformity, and earth's only love is the sun, her 'lusty paramour'. Christina Rossetti changes the tone altogether and prepares, in the coming of Christ, for the marriage of heaven and earth, a deeper and fuller affirmation of the earth's dignity than the Puritan Milton could allow and so a fuller redemption.

For though Christmas celebrates Christ coming as an infant, in Rossetti's poem he is also coming as a bridegroom, as she comments in the poem we read on Advent Sunday:

Earth, put on your whitest
Bridal robe of spotless snow:
For Christmas bringeth Jesus,
Brought for us so low.

25 DECEMBER

From **Ode on the Morning of Christ's Nativity**
John Milton

This is the month, and this the happy morn,
Wherein the Son of Heaven's Eternal King,
Of wedded Maid and Virgin Mother born,
Our great redemption from above did bring;
For so the holy sages once did sing,
That he our deadly forfeit should release,
And with his Father work us a perpetual peace.

That glorious form, that light unsufferable,
And that far-beaming blaze of majesty,
Wherewith he wont at Heaven's high council-table
To sit the midst of Trinal Unity,
He laid aside; and, here with us to be,
Forsook the courts of everlasting day,
And chose with us a darksome house of mortal clay.

Say, heavenly Muse, shall not thy sacred vein
Afford a present to the Infant God?
Hast thou no verse, no hymn, or solemn strain,
To welcome him to this his new abode,
Now while the heaven, by the sun's team untrod,
Hath took no print of the approaching light,
And all the spangled host keep watch in squadrons bright?

See, how from far, upon the eastern road,
The star-led wisards haste with odours sweet:
O run, prevent them with thy humble ode,
And lay it lowly at his blessed feet;
Have thou the honour first thy Lord to greet,
And join thy voice unto the Angel quire,
From out his secret altar touch'd with hallow'd fire.

THE HYMN
It was the winter wild,
While the heaven-born child
All meanly wrapt in the rude manger lies;
Nature, in awe to him,
Had doff'd her gaudy trim,
With her great Master so to sympathize:
It was no season then for her
To wanton with the sun, her lusty paramour.

Only with speeches fair
She wooes the gentle air
To hide her guilty front with innocent snow;
And on her naked shame,
Pollute with sinful blame,
The saintly veil of maiden white to throw;
Confounded, that her Maker's eyes
Should look so near upon her foul deformities.

But he, her fears to cease,
Sent down the meek-ey'd Peace;
She, crown'd with olives green, came softly sliding
Down through the turning sphere,
His ready harbinger,
With turtle wing the amorous clouds dividing;
And, waving wide her myrtle wand,
She strikes an universal peace through sea and land.

Nor war, or battle's sound,
Was heard the world around:
The idle spear and shield were high up hung;
The hooked chariot stood
Unstain'd with hostile blood;
The trumpet spake not to the armed throng;
And kings sat still with awful eye,
As if they surely knew their sovran Lord was by.

But peaceful was the night,
Wherein the Prince of light
His reign of Peace upon the earth began:
The winds, with wonder whist,
Smoothly the waters kiss,
Whispering new joys to the mild ocean,
Who now hath quite forgot to rave,
While birds of calm sit brooding on the charmed wave.

The stars, with deep amaze,
Stand fix'd in steadfast gaze,
Bending one way their precious influence;
And will not take their flight,
For all the morning light,
Or Lucifer, that often warn'd them thence;
But in their glimmering orbs did glow,
Until their Lord himself bespake, and bid them go.

And, though the shady gloom
Had given day her room,
The sun himself withheld his wonted speed,
And hid his head for shame,
As his inferiour flame
The new-enlighten'd world no more should need;
He saw a greater sun appear
Than his bright throne, or burning axletree, could bear.

The shepherds on the lawn,
Or e'er the point of dawn,
Sat simply chatting in a rustick row;
Full little thought they then,
That the mighty Pan
Was kindly come to live with them below;
Perhaps their loves, or else their sheep,
Was all that did their silly thoughts so busy keep.

When such musick sweet
Their hearts and ears did greet,
As never was by mortal finger strook;
Divinely-warbled voice
Answering the stringed noise,
As all their souls in blissful rapture took:
The air, such pleasure loth to lose,
With thousand echoes still prolongs each heavenly close.

Nature that heard such sound,
Beneath the hollow round
Of Cynthia's seat, the aery region thrilling,
Now was almost won
To think her part was done,
And that her reign had here its last fulfilling;
She knew such harmony alone
Could hold all Heaven and Earth in happier union.

At last surrounds their sight
A globe of circular light,
That with long beams the shamefac'd night array'd;
The helmed Cherubim,
And sworded Seraphim,
Are seen in glittering ranks with wings display'd,
Harping in loud and solemn quire,
With unexpressive notes, to Heaven's new-born Heir.

Such musick (as 'tis said)
Before was never made,
But when of old the sons of morning sung,
While the Creator Great
His constellations set,
And the well-balanc'd world on hinges hung;
And cast the dark foundations deep,
And bid the weltering waves their oozy channel keep.

Ring out, ye crystal spheres,
Once bless our human ears,
If ye have power to touch our senses so;
And let your silver chime
Move in melodious time;
And let the base of Heaven's deep organ blow;
And, with your ninefold harmony,
Make up full consort to the angelick symphony.

For, if such holy song
Enwrap our fancy long,
Time will run back, and fetch the age of gold;
And speckled Vanity
Will sicken soon and die,
And leprous Sin will melt from earthly mould;
And Hell itself will pass away,
And leave her dolorous mansions to the peering day.

Yea, Truth and Justice then
Will down return to men,
Orb'd in a rainbow; and, like glories wearing,
Mercy will sit between,
Thron'd in celestial sheen,
With radiant feet the tissued clouds down steering;
And Heaven, as at some festival,
Will open wide the gates of her high palace hall.

It was just before dawn on Christmas Day in 1629 that the young Milton, aged only 21, composed this beautiful ode. This is Milton long before his blindness, before the bitter and disputatious pamphleteering of the Civil War, and before the great polyphonic construction of that grand style in which he uttered *Paradise Lost*. This is Milton still loving and drawing from Spenser, delighting in Shakespeare and the comedies of Ben Jonson; learned certainly, but wearing that learning with a light touch, and flinging out his classical allusions with a kind of frolic. The whole poem is 244 lines long; here I have given the full 'Spenserian prologue' and enough verses of the Hymn to give you a sense of its music and its theology, including the justly famous celebration of the music of the spheres.

Milton borrows from Spenser the long concluding line of each of these opening stanzas, with six stresses instead of five, and uses them to great musical and theological effect, making these lines continuously ring with redemption and good news. The shorter 'That he our deadly forfeit should release' is rounded with the long, strong and in every sense perpetual declaration of the peace of Christ: 'And with his Father work us a perpetual peace'. Indeed, the working of peace and the renewing of relationships is one of the poem's great themes. The second stanza, which deals with the kenosis we have contemplated in several poems this Advent, may well be borrowing from, and in many way improves upon, Spenser's 'Hymne of Heavenly Love' (see 7 December). As Milton tells us:

That glorious form ...
He laid aside; and, here with us to be,
Forsook the courts of everlasting day,
And chose with us a darksome house of mortal clay.

The haunting and elegiac 'darksome house of mortal clay' is certainly an improvement on Spenser's 'fleshly slime'. And it is this famous line of Milton's that may have inspired Edmund Waller's beautiful lines that we read on 9 December:

The soul's dark cottage, batter'd and decay'd,
Lets in new light through chinks that Time hath made ...

Milton concludes his prologue with the lovely image of the poet
rushing along the road to Bethlehem, trying to get ahead of the
wise men ('prevent them' means to go before or ahead of them,
not to stop them) in order to bring his poem and lay it at the feet
of the Christ-child before the gold and frankincense and myrrh
arrive.

Then comes the Hymn itself. In Milton's poem, everything is
alive, and all that we might now reduce to a mere 'it' is a 'thou';
everything is person. The traditional winter snows are not a mere
phenomenon of weather but a 'saintly veil of maiden white' that
blushing nature throws over herself at the thought of her Maker
coming so close. Then comes a lovely vision of peace, in which
Milton draws on the tradition of the *Pax Romana*, the idea that
at the moment of Christ's birth there was no war anywhere in the
world. This was seen as a fulfilment of Isaiah 2.4: 'He shall judge
between the nations, and shall arbitrate for many peoples; and
they shall beat their swords into ploughshares, and their spears
into pruning hooks; nation shall not lift up sword against nation,
neither shall they learn war any more.' For even Peace here is a
person, beautifully realized in verse: 'meek-ey'd',

crown'd with olives green ... softly sliding
Down through the turning sphere,
... the amorous clouds dividing.

There is an almost Keatsean sensuality in early Milton, which
comes as a surprise to those who only know *Paradise Lost*. The
peace is not only between peoples:

Nor war, or battle's sound,
Was heard the world around

but within nature herself, embodied in the lovely long line 'While
birds of calm sit brooding on the charmed wave'. Having set the

scene, he introduces us to the shepherds, and at the same time slips in a highly significant theological idea with some contemporary resonance:

> The shepherds on the lawn,
> Or e'er the point of dawn,
> Sat simply chatting in a rustick row;
> Full little thought they then,
> That the mighty Pan
> Was kindly come to live with them below.

Later on in this poem, Milton shows Christ overcoming the old pagan gods and, as it were, cleansing their temples. But here he introduces a more subtle and profound idea, that in some sense Christ fulfils, clarifies and brings to perfection whatever was good or true in the pagan religion. The shepherds of classical tradition worship Pan, and in some sense, if we can understand it, it is the mighty Pan that has come to them. This idea has been taken up more recently in a famous song by The Waterboys, 'The Return of Pan', which contains the lines:

> At sea in a ship in a thunderstorm
> The very night that Christ was born
> The sailors heard from overhead
> A mighty voice call, 'Pan is dead'.

> So follow Christ as best you can,
> 'Pan is dead, long live Pan'.

There is, I think, a fully Christian sense in which we can sing the chorus of that song:

> The great God Pan is alive!

Then comes the great evocation of the music of the spheres for which this ode is most famous, and which concludes our extract this Christmas morning. Here Milton suggests that it was in and through divine music that the world itself was made, and that if we could hear such music again we would ourselves be remade and eternal. And introducing this Orphic and Pythagorean motif he nevertheless suggests the deepest of Christian themes: the redemption of the world. We also feel, especially in the creation passage in stanza 12, the beginning of that great and sublime vision he was to achieve in the account of creation in *Paradise Lost*:

> Such musick (as 'tis said)
> Before was never made,
> But when of old the sons of morning sung,
> While the Creator Great
> His constellations set,
> And the well-balanc'd world on hinges hung;
> And cast the dark foundations deep,
> And bid the weltering waves their oozy channel keep.

Then, from stanzas 13 through to 15, the end of our extract, comes the musical cry for that music to be heard again, addressing the spheres themselves as they turn, a ringing cry in every sense. Those echoes Tennyson heard and repeated, as we shall see on New Year's Day.

> Ring out, ye crystal spheres,
> Once bless our human ears,
> If ye have power to touch our senses so;
> And let your silver chime
> Move in melodious time;
> And let the base of Heaven's deep organ blow;
> And, with your ninefold harmony,
> Make up full consort to the angelick symphony.

Milton's poetry has been described as itself a kind of organ music, and he certainly plays with that image here. Though C. S. Lewis, in a very perceptive comment in his *Preface to Paradise Lost*, suggests that we ourselves, as we read Milton, in all the height and depth of our sensibility, become the organ on which the music of the poem is played.

While seeming to describe his own imagination he must actually arouse ours, and arouse it not to make definite pictures, but to find again in our own depth the Paradisal light of which all explicit images are only the momentary reflection. We are his organ: when he appears to be describing Paradise he is in fact drawing out the Paradisal Stop in us. (p. 49)

As Milton develops the vision that this music, once heard, might achieve, he makes Christmas Day a window onto our most profound Advent hope: the fulfilment and redemption of all things, the final liberation promised by God. He suggests it in the image of the broken prison and the opened gate, the end of hell:

And Hell itself will pass away,
And leave her dolorous mansions to the peering day.

His poem has taken us from the child 'meanly wrapped in the rude manger' to a transformative vision of the joy and glory he came to give us.

26 DECEMBER

Song of the Shepherds *Richard Bauckham*

We were familiar with the night.
We knew its favourite colours,
its sullen silence
and its small, disturbing sounds,
its unprovoked rages,
its savage dreams.

We slept by turns,
attentive to the flock.
We said little.
Night after night, there was little to say.
But sometimes one of us,
skilled in that way,
would pipe a tune of how things were for us.

They say that once, almost before time,
the stars with shining voices
serenaded
the new born world.
The night could not contain their boundless praise.

We thought that just a poem –
until the night
a song of solar glory,
unutterable, unearthly,
eclipsed the luminaries of the night,
as though the world were exorcised of dark
and, coming to itself, began again.

Later we returned to the flock.
The night was ominously black.
The stars were silent as the sheep.
Nights pass, year on year.
We clutch our meagre cloaks against the cold.
Our ageing piper's fumbling fingers play,
night after night,
an earthly echo of the song that banished dark.
It has stayed with us.

At several points in this anthology I have experimented in juxta-posing a well-known classical poem from 'the canon' written in a previous age and a contemporary poem that addresses the same themes and images, but framed and articulated for the world we live in now, taking up into the music of poetry the ordinary words with which we are familiar. We saw this with Donne's 'Annunci-ation' set against Scott Cairns' 'Annunciation', and Luci Shaw's 'Kenosis' beside Spenser's 'Hymne of Heavenly Love'; so now we read Richard Bauckham's quiet and poignant meditation on the shepherds in light of Milton's great ode.

Wonderful as Milton's poem is, one can't help hearing a slightly patrician and patronizing attitude in the clever young Cambridge undergraduate, as in the line about 'shepherds on the lawn ... simply chatting in a rustick row'. Not so with Richard Bauck-ham. Despite being one of the world's foremost New Testament scholars, in this poem he is not looking down from the ivory tower; rather he uses the full resources of his learning as a scholar and his imagination as a poet to get right inside the shepherds' experience and help us see things from their point of view. The narrative framing of the poem in the first person plural includes us; from the opening word, 'We', we are there. Bauckham does not rush to the moment of revelation, the all-transforming music that will be the point at which his poem and Milton's most com-pletely connect and echo one another. He builds the scene for us quietly and patiently, the very form of the poem imitating the long, mostly silent and uneventful nights that are the shepherds' context. Though perhaps the very tense and tone of those opening lines,

We were familiar with the night.
We knew its favourite colours,
its sullen silence

is preparing us by implicit contrast for the revelation which is to
come. In the second stanza, the lines

We said little.
Night after night, there was little to say

not only set the scene but also introduce an echo we will catch in
the final stanza, when the phrase 'night after night' occurs again,
but transformed. And so the music which is the true subject of this
poem, the song of the shepherds, is first introduced in an unre-
marked and untransformed way, a quiet, skilful, worldly music
that just reflects back what we already know:

But sometimes one of us,
skilled in that way,
would pipe a tune of how things were for us.

Then, the third stanza begins the transformation of both image
and language. Bauckham's scholarship is quietly at work here,
as he asks us to imagine how the shepherds might have recalled
the mediated knowledge of some passages of scripture. The lines
behind this stanza are two particular passages of scripture, from
Job (38.4, 7):

Where were you when I laid the foundation of the earth?...
when the morning stars sang together,
and all the heavenly beings shouted for joy?

and Psalm 19.1–2:

The heavens are telling the glory of God;
and the firmament proclaims his handiwork.
Day to day pours forth speech,
and night to night declares knowledge.

But Bauckham knows that the shepherds, who because their occupation was ritually unclean were excluded from much of the religious life of Israel, would not have the training or education to know and quote these verses directly, or be able to cite their scriptural origins. Nevertheless, they have been formed by a culture that remembers such images, and so even without the direct citation they have imaginative access; the scriptural insight comes down to them almost as folklore and oral tradition, introduced by that phrase 'they say':

> They say that once, almost before time,
> the stars with shining voices
> serenaded
> the new born world.
> The night could not contain their boundless praise.

Then from this evocation of folk memory we are brought into the illuminated and illuminating present moment, as the shepherds suddenly hear and encounter the reality that lay behind their half-remembered scriptures:

> We thought that just a poem –
> until the night
> a song of solar glory,
> unutterable, unearthly,
> eclipsed the luminaries of the night,
> as though the world were exorcised of dark
> and, coming to itself, began again.

And here the language lifts towards the sublime in words like 'solar', 'unutterable', 'unearthly', 'luminaries'. Those last two lines of the stanza take us directly back to Milton's ode and the sense of redemptive renewal which he evoked:

> For, if such holy song
> Enwrap our fancy long,
> Time will run back, and fetch the age of gold.

In both poems something glorious is opened up for us; we glimpse a possibility, but the moment for it is not yet come, and it is sealed up again. As Milton comments in the stanza that follows yesterday's extract:

> But wisest Fate sayes no,
> This must not yet be so.

In Bauckham we get a quiet return to where we started: the stars that once sung silent again, the night seemingly black as ever. Together these poems offer us the experience George Herbert described back at the beginning of Advent in 'The Glance': 'A mirth but open'd and seal'd up again'. And yet, as with the Herbert poem, even the brief opening of that mirth really does change things, and the world to which we return after the vision is not quite so untransfigured as it seems. And this is very delicately suggested in the conclusion of Richard Bauckham's poem. These lines might suggest that even after the vision nothing has changed, echoing as they do the earlier stanzas,

> We clutch our meagre cloaks against the cold.
> Our ageing piper's fumbling fingers play,
> night after night,

but it is not so. The ageing piper may still be playing with fumbling fingers against the cold and dark, but he is playing a new song:

> an earthly echo of the song that banished dark.
> It has stayed with us.

In some ways, this is all we have been doing this Advent, and our whole keeping of Christmas: listening for, attuning ourselves to, and continuing the 'earthly echo of the song that banished dark'.

27 DECEMBER

Nativity *Scott Cairns*

As you lean in, you'll surely apprehend
the tiny God is wrapped
in something more than swaddle. The God

is tightly bound within
His blesséd mother's gaze – her face declares
that *she* is rapt by what

she holds, beholds, reclines beholden to.
She cups His perfect head
and kisses Him, that even here the radiant

compass of affection
is announced, that even here our several
histories converge and slip,

just briefly, out of time. Which is much of what
an icon works as well,
and this one offers up a broad array

of separate narratives
whose temporal relations quite miss the point,
or meet there. Regardless,

one blithe shepherd offers music to the flock,
and – just behind him – there
he is again, and sore afraid, attended

by a trembling companion
and addressed by Gabriel. Across the ridge,
three wise men spur three horses

towards a star, and bowing at the icon's
nearest edge, these same three
yet adore the seated One whose mother serves

as throne. Meantime, stumped,
the kindly Abba Joseph ruminates,
receiving consolation

from an attentive dog whose master may
yet prove to be a holy
messenger disguised as fool. Overhead,

the famous star is all
but out of sight by now; yet, even so,
it aims a single ray

directing our slow pilgrims to the core
where all the journeys meet,
appalling crux and hallowed cave and womb,

where crouched among these other
lowing cattle at their trough, our travelers
receive that creatured air, and pray.

Today we return to Scott Cairns, whose beautiful and densely concentrated poem 'Annunciation' did so much to set the scene at the beginning of Advent. In this poem, 'Nativity', one of a pair of poems called 'Two Icons', he invites us to come with him to Mary and the Christ-child by opening up for us the window of an icon of the nativity.

From its opening lines the poem is immediately close, intense and intimate; annihilating distance, it draws us in:

As you lean in, you'll surely apprehend
the tiny God is wrapped
in something more than swaddle.

Cairns' choice of the word 'apprehend' is perfect, and perhaps
deliberately echoes Shakespeare's reflection on poetry, that
imagination,

apprehends
more than cool reason ever comprehends ...
That if it would but apprehend some joy,
It comprehends some bringer of that joy.
(*A Midsummer Night's Dream*, Act V, Scene 1)

Cairns is certainly using the poetic imagination to the full in order
to invite our apprehension and bring us, image by image, a little
closer to comprehending the bringer of our joy. From the outset
we are in the grip of the enlightening paradox of Incarnation,
there in the juxtaposition of 'tiny' and 'God'; and the whole poem
opens out the vital phrase he introduces in this third line, 'some-
thing more'. It is the purpose of poetry to show us something we
think we already know, and in that showing, show us 'something
more'.

So, having introduced the familiar image of the babe wrapped
in swaddle, Cairns goes on:

The God

is tightly bound within
His blessèd mother's gaze – her face declares
that *she* is rapt by what

she holds, beholds, reclines beholden to.

The language is at once rich and playful, with the idea of Mary's
'gaze' as almost a 'gauze' that wraps its beloved object, and then
the reversal and play on 'rapt': she is 'wrapped' in that she is
bound by him, and 'rapt' by what she holds in love, giving it

rapt attention. Then comes the lovely, musical tolling and play with 'hold': 'she holds', 'beholds', 'reclines beholden to'; we move through the senses from the physical holding to the visual beholding to the spiritual state of being beholden, itself paradoxically something into which we can recline and rest. And all this use of the English word 'hold', 'behold' gently reminds us of the Latin root in 'apprehend': 'to be prehensive', meaning 'to take hold'. And who apprehends, who takes hold here? Mary certainly, but no less certainly we behold, we apprehend, through her. She is the icon or window through which we look at Christ, beholding and beholden, as the first line makes clear. This poem is ultimately not about the look of those presented in the icon, looking at Christ, but is an invitation to look deeply into these things ourselves. So Cairns continues his lucid description of the icon through which he wishes us to see, and we become aware of a sense of a continued Annunciation. Mary's face *declares* something; a radiant compass of affection is *announced*. Let's look at this language in detail:

> She cups His perfect head
> and kisses Him, that even here the radiant
>
> compass of affection
> is announced, that even here our several
> histories converge and slip,
>
> just briefly, out of time.

There is something remarkable going on in the phrase 'the radiant compass of affection', and again Cairns is availing himself of the latent semantic energies stored up in familiar words. In one sense the phrase 'compass of affection' implies 'coming within the compass' of or being compassed around by something, indeed perhaps carrying an echo and a redemptive reply to Shakespeare's famous image of our mortality:

Love's not Times fool, though rosy lips and cheeks
Within his bending sickle's compass come.
(Sonnet 116)

But here we are brought not to the compass of time's 'bending
sickle' but to the radiant compass of that divine affection that
will, in Herbert's phrase, 'look us out of pain'; and even as we
look at this icon, 'slip' us 'briefly, out of time'. But 'the radiant
compass of affection' surely also encompasses the other meaning
of the word: the instrument that gives you true direction, a new
orientation. In the renewed love between God and man, which
Christ brings, we are free, even in the 'dark night of the soul', to
follow the radiant compass of affection.

After this intense concentration on the central exchange
between Mary and Christ at the heart of this nativity icon, Cairns
pans back and shows us the bigger picture in which the nativity
is framed, showing how it 'offers up a broad array of separate
narratives' among which we now know will be our own. For as
we will see, 'our several histories' converge upon this icon, upon
this 'still point of the turning world'.

In the verses that follow, Cairns draws our attention to an
interesting feature of the icon he is describing. The familiar cast of
a nativity scene – the shepherds, the wise men, the angel, Joseph –
are represented more than once as the icon writer depicts various
stages on their journeys, different points of understanding and
revelation. So the same shepherd is shown both regardless, blithe,
playing only to his sheep, and then sore afraid, standing just
behind himself, as it were, trembling, open to the angel's message.
Likewise the three wise men, not yet enlightened, spur their horses
towards a distant star; but also, 'at the icon's nearest edge', adore
Christ enthroned on his mother's lap. The icon itself, with Christ
the alpha and omega at its centre, who comes 'in the fullness of
time' (Galatians 4.4–7), somehow draws all these disparate times
together; even the times when we have 'missed the point' are
pointedly brought into this sacred space to be redeemed. It is as
though, even in the moment when we are most 'regardless', our
'rapt', enlightened self, truly beholding, is standing just behind us.

And so, having panned out to include all our separate narratives and temporal relations, the focus of the poem returns again to its centre, bringing us with it, ourselves pilgrims brought by Cairns' poetic imagination,

> to the core
> where all the journeys meet,
> appalling crux and hallowed cave and womb

And this is the crux of the poem, in every sense. Cairns allows context to bring into focus the hidden cross, embedded in that casual Latin word *crux*. Like Luci Shaw's 'Kenosis', this poem does not sentimentalize the nativity into some baby-worshipping Christmas-card vision of niceness; it takes us to the crux of the matter, to what it was the Christ-child came to do in us, through us and for us at Calvary. Even as we behold, we are indeed beholden and our only true response is to 'receive that creatured air, and pray'.

28 DECEMBER

Refugee *Malcolm Guite*

We think of him as safe beneath the steeple,
Or cosy in a crib beside the font,
But he is with a million displaced people
On the long road of weariness and want.
For even as we sing our final carol
His family is up and on that road,
Fleeing the wrath of someone else's quarrel,
Glancing behind and shouldering their load.
Whilst Herod rages still from his dark tower
Christ clings to Mary, fingers tightly curled,
The lambs are slaughtered by the men of power,
And death squads spread their curse across the world.
But every Herod dies, and comes alone
To stand before the Lamb upon the throne.

I noted in yesterday's commentary the danger of sentimentalizing, and so trivializing, the nativity scene. As our houses are deluged in a cascade of cosy Christmas images, glittery frosted cards and happy, holy families who seem to be remarkably comfortable in strangely clean stables, we can lose track of the essential gospel truth: that the world into which God chose to be born for us was then, as now, fraught with danger and menace. Indeed, we will not understand the light that shines at Christmas if we remove the dark backdrop. Richard Bauckham's 'Song of the Shepherds' restores it for us in the line 'The night was ominously black'; but Christina Rossetti set the scene on Advent Sunday with 'midnight, black as pitch'; Herbert, even in the midst of his joyful 'Glance', reminded us of 'malicious and ill-meaning harm'; Donne's 'Annunciation' spoke of 'death's force'; Luci Shaw reminded us of 'the felt rebuff ... the lash ... the sad heart of the human race'. And today's commemoration, the Feast of the Holy Innocents, brings home with full force what might be called 'the shadow side' of the Christian story.

The story of Herod's jealous rage and the massacre of the innocents would be too appalling to bear were we not called upon to contemplate it almost every day in the news. What Herod did then is still being done across the world by tyrants who would sooner kill innocent people than lose their grip on power. We are still reeling from the appalling slaughter of children in Peshawar by the Pakistani Taliban, as well as the continued violence, much of it directed towards children, by Islamic State in Syria and Iraq. This scarred and wounded world is the one into which Jesus was born, the world he came to save; among those brought by his blood through the grave and gate of death to the bliss of heaven are those children of Bethlehem who died for his name without ever knowing him. But he knows them, as he knows and loves every child in Syria, Iraq and Pakistan, and he says of them, to every Herod, 'as you did it to one of the least of these who are members of my family, you did it to me' (Matthew 25.40).

In this sonnet I have followed the narrative in Matthew 2.13–18, which goes out of its way to mention the death of Herod. The story of the flight into Egypt seems utterly contemporary. If we acknowledge the idea of kenosis – the self-emptying of God – then we must contemplate the experience of the Christ-child as being exactly the same as that of the disturbed and bewildered children we see being carried by their mothers in desperation out of war zones. These children cannot possibly know the cause of the quarrel that has destroyed their homes; they could not name or articulate the label that has made them enemies of the state; utterly innocent of the long, hideous adult agenda that has visited such devastation upon them, they are 'fleeing the wrath of someone else's quarrel'. Likewise if we are to take seriously Christ's teaching at the end of Matthew, the same Gospel that gave us this appalling story – that he is really and substantially in the lives and bodies of those who are oppressed, and whatsoever is done to them is done to him – then we must become aware that the risen Christ is still a refugee. But this is not to despair. It means that we can still meet him and help him in his need. We cannot turn back through time to meet the holy family as they fled through the deserts of Egypt, but we can certainly meet them now. And there is one more thing I tried to draw out in this sonnet. There is a judgement, there is finally an accountability, and thank God, it is a judgement with mercy. Perhaps the most profound and paradoxical image in the whole of scripture is that of the Lamb upon the throne. We should never cease to be astonished by that verse:

> for the Lamb at the centre of the throne will be their
>   shepherd,
> and he will guide them to springs of the water of life,
> and God will wipe away every tear from their eyes.
> (Revelation 7.17)

The entire edifice of scripture up to this point has been predicated on the difference between the shepherd and the sheep. 'All we like sheep have gone astray' (Isaiah 53.6). God is figured in the Old and New Testament as the transcendent shepherd, in that sense utterly different in kind from the sheep. But this verse of Revelation reveals one more meaning of Christmas, of Incarnation. We have a shepherd who knows what it is like to be a lamb. He has himself been one of the vulnerable flock, he has been misled by false shepherds, and made victim of the wolf. And that is why he is able to wipe away the tears from our eyes, because he himself has wept them. What might this mean for the Herods of this world? It certainly means that they will face judgement; they will meet their victims in Christ and Christ in their victims, and know and have to acknowledge to the core what they have done. In that final light there will be no evasion, no spin, no propaganda, no polite euphemisms, but only searing truth. But right at the heart of the truth will be the Lamb, who died as much for the

Herods as for their victims; and even there 'the need and chance to salvage everything', the possibility in repentance, for the blood-thirsty themselves, to be 'washed ... in the blood of the Lamb' (Revelation 7.14).

29 DECEMBER

For Our Lady of Guadalupe *Grevel Lindop*

The taxi windscreen's broken,
lightning-starred with a crack from one corner:
signature of a stone from the Oaxaca road.
It drops me by the shanty-town of stalls
where I will buy her plastic image later –
garish, I hope, and cheap,
for kitsch is authenticity.

A jagged rift of space
splits the old basilica's perfect Baroque,
an intricately-cracked stone egg
atilt on sliding subsoil where the Aztec
city's lake was carelessly filled in.
Crowds pass its listing shell without a glance,
heading for the concrete-and-stained-glass

swirl that mimics
Juan Diego's cloak, where she appeared
and painted her own image on the fabric
to show sceptical bishops
how perfect love could visit a poor Indian
after the wars, and fill his cloak with roses.
Now the cloak's under glass behind the altar.

A priest celebrates Mass,
but we walk round the side

to queue for the moving pavement that will take us closer,
its mechanical glide into the dark
floating us past the sacred cloth
and her miraculous, soft, downcast gaze:
not Spanish and not Indian but both,

lovely *mestiza* Virgin, reconciler
who stands against the flashbulbs' irregular
pizzicato of exploding stars,
and while we slide on interlocking steel
opens for us her mantle, from which roses
pour and pour in torrents, like blood
from a wound that may never be healed.

For today's poem we return to the writing of the contemporary English poet Grevel Lindop. Early in Advent we considered his 'secular' love poem 'The Moons' (2 December), in which he wanted to make the light in the darkness a gift for the beloved who had pointed out that light. And even in that secular giving we felt some sense of a transcendent light shining through. So too in today's poem, about a visit to the popular shrine of Our Lady of Guadalupe in Mexico, there is a profound, perhaps almost reluctant, movement through the secular to the sacred, a series of unasked but nonetheless transformative epiphanies.

We start with the vivid and the particular, indeed the plastic and the cheap, the cracked and broken down, but even here there are hints that something else is going on. If we have eyes, the star of the nativity is unexpectedly shining: 'lightning-starred' in the cracked taxi window, and 'exploding stars' in the reflected flashbulbs of the faithful. As we arrive with Lindop in the crack-screened taxi in a poor Mexican 'shanty-town of stalls', this could so easily have been a different poem, fitting into that genre of travel writing in which the sophisticated westerner gives an apparently empathetic but ultimately detached and condescending account of other people's customs. We could have been invited, at least implicitly, to sneer at and feel superior to the tacky plastic, peasant Catholic religious kitsch, or to tut and raise our eyebrows at people who have neglected their lovely old baroque basilica, letting it slide into ruin while they pour into the inferior ritziness of concrete and stained glass. In such an alternative poem, the mechanical walkway of 'interlocking steel', gliding mindless tourists or the gullible superstitious past some glassed-in, faked attraction, would have been the last straw, and we would feel rather smugly that the National Trust manages our heritage with much more taste and style. But, thanks be to God, this is not the poem Lindop has given us. Instead, he takes us on a journey into humility, empathy and a strange authenticity, as in the key, paradoxical line that concludes the first verse: 'for kitsch is authenticity'. We know too, from this first verse, that this mind-changing journey is one the poet himself has to make himself. Those lines,

where I *will buy* her plastic image *later* –
garish, I hope, and cheap,

are highly significant, implying that when he first arrived he might have disdained the stalls of plastic images. Only after his actual encounter with Our Lady of Guadalupe does he understand their value, and comes back to buy one. What does it mean in this context to say that 'kitsch is authenticity'? In one sense, kitsch, like beauty, is in the eye of the beholder. To call something kitsch is to strike an attitude of superiority, and to presume we know how other people see the same object. What we learn on the journey of this poem is that the devotion of the poor may transfigure cracked and broken, even poor and shoddy material more effectively than the finesse and fine taste of the sceptical rich. Though his wound 'may never be healed', it comes to us, as to Juan Diego, in a gift not of blood but of roses.

So in the second verse, the journey begins. Past the 'listing shell' of the old basilica, heading for 'the concrete-and-stained-glass' again, Lindop is playing with our expectation. By ending the line and stanza with 'the concrete-and-stained-glass', in contradistinction to 'the old basilica's perfect Baroque' we might be teased into thinking that the crowds are passing by the empty shell of a church in order to flock to the concrete and stained glass

of a shopping centre, as happens every Christmas in the scep-
tical West. But no, the stanza is at an end, but the sentence is
not finished. The glass is a glass 'swirl' that mimics the cloak of
the poor Mexican Indian peasant to whom was vouchsafed an
epiphany greater than any offered to sceptical European bishops.
Our Lady becomes the unexpected and radical visitant of perfect
love, pouring her roses of consolation into the cloaks of the poor.
Even as he rides the tourist's 'mechanical glide', something in the
poet, and so in us, is being transformed and opened up. He has
prepared us for this, first in the image of the cracked windscreen
and then in the 'jagged rift of space' that 'splits the old basilica';
and now in the gaze of the Madonna there is a deeper opening
still. She 'opens for us her mantle' and that act becomes an open-
ing of the deep wound in the world – the wound that made the
wars, that divided Spanish and Indian, the wound of our fallen
nature. But somehow, in and behind that, the other wound is
opened. We think of the sword that pierced Mary's heart, the
wound of God's compassion opened in the side of Jesus, from
which blood pours not in condemnation but in healing. And all
this is somehow apprehended by someone who does not yet cele-
brate or participate in it, yet equally cannot ignore it. The poet is
delicate in placing himself to one side,

A priest celebrates Mass,
but we walk round the side

And yet in spite of everything, something has been vouchsafed,
and we know he will return to the shanty-town to buy her plastic
image, having learnt a lesson in authenticity.

30 DECEMBER

Christmas (I) *George Herbert*

After all pleasures as I rid one day,
My horse and I, both tir'd, bodie and minde,
With full crie of affections, quite astray,
I took up in the next inne I could finde,
There when I came, whom found I but my deare,
My dearest Lord, expecting till the grief
Of pleasures brought me to him, readie there
To be all passengers most sweet relief?
O Thou, whose glorious, yet contracted light,
Wrapt in night's mantle, stole into a manger;
Since my dark soul and brutish is thy right,
To Man of all beasts be not thou a stranger:
Furnish & deck my soul, that thou mayst have
A better lodging than a rack or grave.

Milton's 'Ode on the Morning of Christ's Nativity', written more
or less contemporaneously with this poem of Herbert's, gave us
the lovely idea of the poet hastening to get ahead of the wise men
and come to the inn himself. Likewise, Scott Cairns' 'Nativity'
invited us to come to the inn and the manger ourselves. Here
Herbert gives that perhaps conventionally pious idea of journey-
ing in great devotion to the inn at Bethlehem an entirely new twist
with a kind of fierce honesty, for the protagonist in Herbert's
poem is not in the least devout. He couldn't care less about put-
ting the Christ back into Christmas. He is simply riding 'after
all pleasures'. The great thing about this poem is that he comes

to Christ, quite accidentally and unintentionally, just putting up at the nearest inn, only to find that all this time Christ has been expecting him with the full and ancient sense of *expectio*: that is to say, 'looking out'. It is one thing for us, in our own time and piously, to choose to behold the icon. It's quite another to know that all the time the icon is beholding and expecting us, patiently awaiting our arrival. So the octet of the sonnet sets the scene for this encounter:

> After all pleasures as I rid one day,
> My horse and I, both tir'd, bodie and minde,
> With full crie of affections, quite astray

Herbert aptly catches the experience even of a modern Christmas in this combination of pleasure and exhaustion, of deliberately riding out and yet also feeling harried and astray. The term 'with full crie of affections' is brilliant. Its immediate context is hunting with hounds, which might be just the kind of pleasure for which a man of Herbert's estate might choose to ride at Christmas. But the table has turned, and Herbert is the hunted. His very affections, undisciplined and in full cry, have brought him to bay, and driven him off his proper course, astray. There is a sense in which he takes up at the next inn to escape the full cry of his pursuing affections, demons, habits or addictions – the dark side of pleasures; or, as Herbert puts it even more sharply and paradoxically, 'the grief of pleasures brought me to him':

> whom found I but my deare,
> My dearest Lord, expecting till the grief
> Of pleasures brought me to him, readie there
> To be all passengers most sweet relief?

This idea, that even for the apparently indifferent man of pleasure the exhaustion, the *tristesse* of satiety, may bring us to Christ, is something Herbert explored in another poem, 'The Pulley', with its beautiful conclusion,

If goodness lead him not, yet weariness
May toss him to my breast.

And when we arrive, over-pleasured, burnt-out, exhausted by our own consumerism, we find that all the time, and by sheer grace, we have kept an appointment; our Lord was waiting patiently for us. Then comes the *volta* between octet and sestet, and everything turns. We are no longer describing a scene from the past in the third person; we are directly addressing Christ in the present:

O Thou, whose glorious, yet contracted light,
Wrapt in night's mantle, stole into a manger.

From this point forward we sense a series of connections with Cairns' 'Nativity': our own arrival at the manger, the play on 'wrapt' and 'mantle', the numbering of ourselves among the beast and the cattle, the intuition of the cross. As so often, Herbert ends his poem with a final twist. For the first 12 lines he is the unexpected yet expected arrival at Christ's inn, and Christ, even in his infancy, his glorious yet contracted light, is host. In the final lines Herbert turns the tables and invites Christ as a guest into his soul, even though he knows that Christ himself must furnish it. As he asks to be able to give Christ a better lodging than 'a rack or grave' there is something very sharp in the language, especially in the choice of the word 'rack'. The cross is an instrument of torture that has been sanitized by piety, worn smooth by devotion, but the rack was in dreadful and legal use in Herbert's England. It was a daring move to invite readers of his day to see Christ Jesus stretched on a contemporary instrument of torture, not a distant cross. Although the poem's last word is 'grave', the movement of the poem does not end there, but with the invitation to the Christ-child into the soul of both narrator and reader.

31 DECEMBER

The Darkling Thrush *Thomas Hardy*

I leant upon a coppice gate
    When Frost was spectre-grey,
And Winter's dregs made desolate
    The weakening eye of day.
The tangled bine-stems scored the sky
    Like strings of broken lyres,
And all mankind that haunted nigh
    Had sought their household fires.

The land's sharp features seemed to be
    The Century's corpse outleant,
His crypt the cloudy canopy,
    The wind his death-lament.
The ancient pulse of germ and birth
    Was shrunken hard and dry,
And every spirit upon earth
    Seemed fervourless as I.

At once a voice arose among
    The bleak twigs overhead
In a full-hearted evensong
    Of joy illimited;
An aged thrush, frail, gaunt, and small,
    In blast-beruffled plume,
Had chosen thus to fling his soul
    Upon the growing gloom.

So little cause for carolings
　　Of such ecstatic sound
Was written on terrestrial things
　　Afar or nigh around,
That I could think there trembled through
　　His happy good-night air
Some blessed Hope, whereof he knew
　　And I was unaware.

This poem, for the last day of the year, reflects the mood of the dying year, the dying century, dying humanity. But paradoxically it is also a poem full of hidden hope. Hardy fully witnesses the bleakness but sets against it the counter-witness of the thrush's song, holding them together with the tentative syntax of his conditional possibility of 'some blessed Hope'. This poem was written on 31 December 1900, and the dying of that winter's day Hardy took to be the century's death: the end of the nineteenth century, with all its hopes of unimpeded progress and universal peace, cheated and defeated.

　The outward and visible desolation of the day becomes, as it were, the first voice of the poem, and Hardy's choice of language for that voice paints a word-picture of decline and dissolution from which one might think there was no recovery: 'spectre-grey ... dregs ... desolate ... weakening ... tangled ... broken ... haunted ... corpse ... crypt ... shrunken ... fervourless ... bleak ... frail ... gaunt ... gloom ...' But then Hardy introduces a second voice:

At once a voice arose among
The bleak twigs overhead
In a full-hearted evensong
Of joy illimited

The language chosen for this voice is drawn not from the realm of death and decay that was the register of the first voice, but from the language of the sacred; it is full of echoes from the Church upon which Hardy thought he had turned his back: 'full-hearted

WAITING ON THE WORD

evensong ... joy ... soul ... carolings ... blessed Hope'. The fact that we hear *both* these voices in this poem, with words from two such distinct linguistic registers being woven together, is a testament to Hardy's integrity and honesty as an artist. It would have been as easy and perhaps tempting to have ignored the witness of the thrush, to have gone home and written an unremittingly grim poem; as, in a similar way, authors of religious doggerel write 'up-beat hymns' that recycle the clichés of hope without ever making contact with the tragedies of life as it is actually lived. Hardy's witness in this poem is that he can neither ignore nor believe the thrush. What he sees as he leans on that gate on a winter day gives him no hope at all, but he is not prepared to limit reality to 'the things that are seen'; and perhaps the most honest word in the poem is 'seemed', at the end of the second stanza. Had he written, 'And every spirit upon earth' *was* 'fervourless as I', he might never have heard the thrush at all; or hearing it, his mind might have twisted its song into yet another symbol of decay.

The first two stanzas are concerned with the outward and visible world, with what we can see; hope comes in the third stanza, when we stop looking at the familiar and listen, suddenly, to the unfamiliar.

But even as Hardy the poet allows the thrush to help him apprehend the possibility of some 'blessed Hope', Hardy the philosopher tries to have the last word, closing the poem with the claim to be 'unaware' of that hope. 'Unaware' is an extraordinary word with which to conclude a poem that is supremely about awareness: awareness of both the signs of mortality and the intimations of immortality. In some ways, this beautiful poem is a testimony against itself. Its tentative syntax is subverted by its ecstatic imagery.

1 JANUARY

In Memoriam CVI *Alfred Lord Tennyson*

Ring out, wild bells, to the wild sky,
  The flying cloud, the frosty light:
  The year is dying in the night;
Ring out, wild bells, and let him die.

Ring out the old, ring in the new,
  Ring, happy bells, across the snow:
  The year is going, let him go;
Ring out the false, ring in the true.

Ring out the grief that saps the mind
  For those that here we see no more;
  Ring out the feud of rich and poor,
Ring in redress to all mankind.

Ring out a slowly dying cause,
  And ancient forms of party strife;
  Ring in the nobler modes of life,
With sweeter manners, purer laws.

Ring out the want, the care, the sin,
  The faithless coldness of the times;
  Ring out, ring out my mournful rhymes
But ring the fuller minstrel in.

Ring out false pride in place and blood,
  The civic slander and the spite;
  Ring in the love of truth and right,
Ring in the common love of good.

Ring out old shapes of foul disease;
  Ring out the narrowing lust of gold;
  Ring out the thousand wars of old,
Ring in the thousand years of peace.

Ring in the valiant man and free,
  The larger heart, the kindlier hand;
  Ring out the darkness of the land,
Ring in the Christ that is to be.

The pealing of bells ringing in the new year brings us round again to Tennyson's great poem *In Memoriam*. On 12 December, we listened with him for the 'muffled peal' of bells heard in grief, whose half-heard chime served only to remind him of his loss. But now, he strikes another note. In the art of English change ringing we hear a wonderful interweaving of bells, each with its own tone and name, changing places in a complex dance, answering one another, constantly changing order to renew and transfigure a pattern. In some ways, this is also how English poetry works. Playing together in the great belfry of the English literary canon and the sounding chamber – what Eliot called 'the auditory imagination' – of their readers' minds, poets echo, summon and interchange one another's movements. So even across the sounding chamber of this small anthology, we know that Tennyson on some Christmas had heard and been lifted by Milton's invocation,

Ring out, ye crystal spheres,
Once bless our human ears,
If ye have power to touch our senses so

and he modulates it into his own opening here, 'Ring out, wild bells, to the wild sky'. The sound of the poem is itself a mimesis of its subject, with its constantly repeated opening, 'ring ... ring ... ring ... ring', and its rhymes and assonance modulating through the sound changes of its bell-like music. Listening to the church bells at Ottery St Mary in his childhood, the young Coleridge had said,

> the old church-tower,
> Whose bells, the poor man's only music, rang
> From morn to evening, all the hot Fair-day,
> So sweetly, that they stirred and haunted me
> With a wild pleasure, falling on mine ear
> Most like articulate sounds of things to come!

Tennyson, who surely knew this passage, takes up in his poem the task of articulating what are those thing to come, of which the bells speak, and centring them surely and clearly on our Advent hope in the coming of Christ; not just at Christmas but in and through all time and at the end.

He sets the scene in the wild sky, in the dying year, and the bells that will ring in the New Year in the familiar ritual. But then, he bodies it forth, with utter clarity, and tells us in no uncertain terms what the old is that must be rung out, the new that must be rung in, both for himself moving beyond grief and for ourselves and our society growing in maturity through Christ. So at a personal level this part of the poem does indeed 'ring out the grief that saps the mind for those that here we see no more', and allows Tennyson to move on from his long grief for Arthur Hallam; this same passage has allowed countless people sense in reading this poem a progression through and from their own grief. But Tennyson is not content to allow poetry to become a merely privatized consolation, an inward subjective fantasy that ignores or compensates for the ills of the world. The bells are hung in public towers and ring out into our common space, and Tennyson calls us to ring them for the common good:

> Ring out the feud of rich and poor,
> Ring in redress to all mankind ...

Ring out the want, the care, the sin,
The faithless coldness of the times;

Again and again, Tennyson rings an alarm bell at the evils of his
own age – the 'false pride in place and blood', 'the civic slander
and the spite', 'the narrowing lust and gold', 'the thousand wars
of old'. When Tennyson was writing, in the mid-nineteenth cen-
tury, there really was an air of hope about gradual progress and
amelioration. It was the age of reform, the age of the Factory
Acts. Public endeavour was genuinely and disinterestedly chang-
ing the social and physical fabric of English life for the good and
to the immense practical improvement of many people's lives. It
was not unnatural to hope that such progress and improvements
would go on indefinitely, that it would be, as he says elsewhere
in the poem, 'a light in darkness' that will 'grow'. And it was not
unreasonable even to hope that a gradual enlightenment would
see an end to 'the thousand wars of old'. Of course, we read the
poem now after the hideous crash of those Victorian dreams of
unimpeded progress, crushed and obliterated in the mechanized
carnage of World War One, 'the war to end all wars' which was
itself the prelude to the world's bloodiest century. Does this mean
that we must abandon the hope expressed in this great passage,
and treat with scorn or scepticism all those whose imaginations
are kindled for the improvement of humankind, who look for
'the larger heart, the kindlier hand'? I don't think so. We may
be tempted to despair, and it is perhaps the easier and certainly
the lazier option. But ultimately, the great and life-transforming
hope of this passage is not rooted in the immediate success of one
scheme of amelioration or another, but in the only place where
hope can be rooted: in Christ himself, and his long Advent. It is
those who know that, however faintly the bell in their hand may
chime, they are ringing in the Christ that is to be who can make
the most fruitful and productive changes in the here and the now.

2 JANUARY

The Bird in the Tree *Ruth Pitter*

The tree, and its haunting bird,
    Are the loves of my heart;
But where is the word, the word,
    Oh where is the art,

To say, or even to see,
    For a moment of time,
What the Tree and the Bird must be
    In the true sublime?

They shine, listening to the soul,
    And the soul replies;
But the inner love is not whole,
    and the moment dies.

Oh give me before I die
    The grace to see
With eternal, ultimate eye,
    The Bird and the Tree.

The song in the living Green,
    The Tree and the Bird –
Oh have they ever been seen,
    Ever been heard?

On New Year's Eve we considered Hardy's almost reluctant glimpse of transfiguration, 'when Frost was spectre-grey', and 'shrunken hard and dry', and his heart, bleak as the world through which he moves, nevertheless heard for a moment the 'ecstatic sound' of his 'darkling thrush'. And even though he wanted to end his poem with the word 'unaware', something of the transcended 'trembled through' his poem. Today's poem, also about hearing a bird in a tree, addresses the question of how the transcendent might for 'a moment of time' tremble through into the immanent.

But unlike Hardy, Ruth Pitter is not reluctant. Indeed, she wishes to be utterly open to the moment and even so she despairs of finding the word, the art, to convey the epiphany. One of the best but most neglected poets of the last century, Ruth Pitter had a distinguished literary career, and a serious engagement with the poets and the issues of her day. Her work was known and valued by Yeats, Thom Gunn and Philip Larkin. She was a friend and correspondent of C. S. Lewis, and may well have exercised considerable influence on his later writing. But unlike Eliot, Pound and Auden, she did not abandon traditional form, and eschewed the self-conscious tropes of modernism, preferring to see how she could renew the old forms and visions inherited from George Herbert and her beloved Thomas Traherne. And it may partly be this refusal to join the modernist mainstream that has led to her neglect, though now in 'postmodernist times' it may assist in her revival.

The heart of Ruth Pitter's poetic vision might be summed up in Herbert's phrase 'heaven in ordinary': not simply that she had the gift to communicate a transfigured vision, and unveil a little of heaven in the ordinary; she believed that there was no ordinary. It was her conviction that the experience of ordinariness was simply a failure of attention, a lazy habit of mind, and she would have agreed with Coleridge that the purpose of poetry is

> awakening the mind's attention from the lethargy of custom, and directing it to the loveliness and the wonders of the world before us; an inexhaustible treasure, but for which, in consequence of the film of familiarity and selfish solicitude we have eyes, yet see not, ears that hear not, and hearts that neither feel nor understand. (*Biographia Literaria*, Chapter 14)

Her question is not, how can I write about this bird and this tree so poetically that for a moment they symbolize the sublime?, but rather, how can I concentrate sufficiently and write with enough exactitude and clarity to see this bird and this tree even for a moment in actual disclosure of their true sublimity?

In a sense her poem starts with Hopkins' experience in seeing 'The Windhover':

> my heart in hiding
> Stirred for a bird ...

Pitter goes beyond the stirring to a direct identity:

> The tree, and its haunting bird,
> Are the loves of my heart ...

She then poses the question that falls across the threshold of every artist and shadows the desk of every writer:

> But where is the word, the word,
> Oh where is the art,
>
> To say, or even to see,
> For a moment of time,
> What the Tree and the Bird must be
> In the true sublime?

And we notice here that the tree and the bird have been capitalized. In some sense, we are dealing now not simply with 'that tree and its haunting bird' but with 'The Tree' and 'The Bird', the true Platonic forms informing and shining through 'that tree' and 'that bird'. As Pitter goes on to say:

> They shine, listening to the soul,
> And the soul replies;
> But the inner love is not whole,
> And the moment dies.

For Pitter, we are both connected and disconnected. There is something in our souls that sings and replies to the bird as it shines in the tree, but at the same time, even as the heart leaps up, the vision fails, for

> the inner love is not whole,
> and the moment dies.

There could be no clearer expression of the fall, the inner woundedness that Christ comes to heal. Indeed, in the next verse Pitter recognizes that the only thing that will heal this breach is grace:

> Oh give me before I die
> The grace to see
> With eternal, ultimate eye,
> The Bird and the Tree.

In some ways we are again in the territory of Herbert's poem 'The Glance'. We've had a momentary glimpse of something given and sealed away again; this sets up in us what Lewis called 'an inconsolable longing' to have the vision again, to heal the breach. So the poem whose first line gave us 'haunting' ends with a haunting refrain and question:

> The song in the living Green,
> The Tree and the Bird –
> Oh have they ever been seen,
> Ever been heard?

From today, we move towards the Feast of Epiphany. Pitter's brief epiphany in this poem and her longing for its completion become a paradigm for all the epiphanies we shall seek and celebrate in this season. In truth, we are not looking for a brief encounter, however sublime, but to pass through that encounter into that state where with 'ultimate eye' we can enjoy the eternal.

3 JANUARY

Courtesy *Hilaire Belloc*

Of Courtesy, it is much less
Than Courage of Heart or Holiness,
Yet in my Walks it seems to me
That the Grace of God is in Courtesy.

On Monks I did in Storrington fall,
They took me straight into their Hall;
I saw Three Pictures on a wall,
And Courtesy was in them all.

The first the Annunciation;
The second the Visitation;
The third the Consolation,
Of God that was Our Lady's Son.

The first was of St. Gabriel;
On Wings a-flame from Heaven he fell;
And as he went upon one knee
He shone with Heavenly Courtesy.

Our Lady out of Nazareth rode –
It was Her month of heavy load;
Yet was her face both great and kind,
For Courtesy was in Her Mind.

The third it was our Little Lord,
Whom all the Kings in arms adored;
He was so small you could not see
His large intent of Courtesy.

Our Lord, that was Our Lady's Son,
Go bless you, People, one by one;
My Rhyme is written, my work is done.

Hilaire Belloc (1870-1953) is best known for his comic and deliciously gruesome poems and cautionary tales for children, although it would be hard to decide whether it's the children themselves or the adults who read to them who get the most pleasure from the outrageous and dreadful fates of Henry King, Matilda and their companions. It is certainly in Belloc's verse that the seeds of the rumbustious and comically exaggerated world of *Charlie and the Chocolate Factory*, with all its grim comeuppances, were sown in the mind of Roald Dahl, a Belloc enthusiast. Belloc is also remembered for his brilliant travel writing, in books like *The Path to Rome* and *The Cruise of the Nona*, his brief, terse and satiric essays, and for his memorable epigrams, such as his famous self-penned epitaph:

When I am dead I hope it may be said
His sins were scarlet and his books were read.

He was, however, a considerable poet beyond his famous modes of comedy and satire, and today's poem is one of many delicate and beautiful pieces that celebrate his deeply held Catholic faith. I have chosen it for the run-up to Epiphany because it is essentially a series of little epiphanies; each of the three pictures are moments of epiphany, or 'showings forth' of the glory of God in scripture. Because of its strong rhythms, chiming rhymes and archaic, ballad-like feel, I had assumed that this poem had some generic medieval setting and we were to imagine the narrator as a *jongleur* or perhaps one of the *vagantes*, the wandering scholars about whom Helen Waddell wrote so beautifully. In fact, it records quite literally and factually what happened on 17 May 1908, the day it was written. The poem's setting is not a medieval fantasy priory but Our Lady of England Priory in Storrington, West Sussex, and the 'monks' who offered Belloc such courteous hospitality were a community of Canons Regular of Prémontré. Though their order was founded in the twelfth century, they had only come to this priory and established it as a shrine in 1902, six years before Belloc visited, so it was in his view quite a contemporary and modern setting. This courteous and hospitable community had a good track record in welcoming and nurturing poets; some years earlier they had given sanctuary and healing to the great poet Francis Thompson when he was recovering from an opium addiction.

Belloc's encomium begins with a rather humble deprecation of courtesy. It opens by proclaiming that other virtues, such as holiness of heart or courage, are greater, but, of course, this act of self-deprecation is the very heart of courtesy, and in some sense, even as he appears to dispraise it, courtesy triumphs. There is also a subtle move being made very gently in this first verse, in the old and long debate between works and grace, as Belloc delicately implies that courage of heart or even holiness might become merely human works, but 'the Grace of God is in Courtesy'. Then he lays out for us the three pictures: the Annunciation, the Visitation and the visit of the wise men, interestingly called here the Consolation. As we have seen in the poetry of John Donne and Scott Cairns, the Annunciation opens out the mystery celebrated at Christmas: the meeting and reconciliation of heaven and earth. Belloc describes not simply a particular painting in Storrington, but the archetypal encounter that is the subject of many medieval paintings and reproduced on countless cards: Gabriel kneeling before Mary. But this poem draws our attention to what an extraordinary image that is. In meetings between angels and human beings in the scriptures, it is usually the human beings who fall down in fear and trembling, who are tempted to worship, or who are simply overcome by the sudden encounter with the numinous; and this is why the angels' opening words are almost always *noli timere*, 'do not be afraid'. Here, all this is turned upside down.

An archangel from the heights of the heavenly hierarchy kneels
courteously and graciously before a young girl from Nazareth;
even in the angel's gesture we see the true depth of the kenosis,
the self-emptying humility with which heaven courteously comes
to reconcile earth. The contemporary poet Gwyneth Lewis, in her
poem 'Annunciation', also writing about a picture of the scene,
ends with that same astonishing image, as she contemplates the
mystery 'that had brought a plain angel to his grateful knees'.

Then comes the Visitation. Belloc's strong rhythms and simple
language somehow bring home a close and compassionate picture
of Mary coping with the pregnancy: 'it was Her month of heavy
load'. And then he gives us a glimpse of her face, and through that
a glimpse into her mind:

> Yet was her face both great and kind,
> For Courtesy was in Her Mind.

The courtesy here is in the visit to Elizabeth, in the young woman
honouring her older kinswoman; in turn, in another reversal, the
kinswoman exclaims, 'And why has this happened to me, that the
mother of my Lord comes to me?' (Luke 1.43). Indeed, one might
even say that there is a further courtesy in the visitation as the
cousins greet one another from the womb; John the Baptist leaps
in Elizabeth's womb to honour Christ in Mary's. I tried to suggest
a little of this in my own poem about the Visitation in *Sounding
the Seasons*:

> Here is a meeting made of hidden joys
> Of lightenings cloistered in a narrow place
> From quiet hearts the sudden flame of praise
> And in the womb the quickening kick of grace.

And then Belloc's third picture prepares us for the great 'show-
ing' we shall celebrate on the Feast of the Epiphany itself on 6
January. Three poets in this anthology have already urged us to
come to the inn along with the kings. Belloc's verse here gently
and delicately adds to our sense of what we might see:

The third it was our Little Lord,
Whom all the Kings in arms adored

There is a deliberate ambiguity about the phrase 'in arms'. In one sense we are invited to think of great stately kings, so moved by the little lord that they take him up in their arms; but we are also to think of them as men 'in arms', who must kneel down, find humility and worship the babe – in stark contrast to those other men in arms who will shortly come seeking to slaughter him. Again, the great background mystery here is kenosis, the courteous self-diminution of love, the notion of immensity choosing to be cloistered. It is all done very simply with plays on 'little', 'small' and 'large'. So first we have the contrast between the 'Little Lord and 'the Kings in arms', then between the smallness of Christ's physical body and his 'large intent on Courtesy', and again we are invited to see the grace of God in this courtesy extended beyond the frame of this little picture. It is not simply that the Christ-child intends courtesy at this moment towards the kings who have come to worship him; his large intent of courtesy reaches out towards us and through every action in his life. Soon we will see the courtesy with which he lays aside his garments, takes the bowl and the towel and washes his disciples' feet; the courtesy with which he carries our load for us; and finally, in the sacrament of Communion, the courtesy with which, in Herbert's words, 'Love bids us welcome'.

4 JANUARY

From **Hymn Before Sunrise, in the Vale of Chamouni**
Samuel Taylor Coleridge

Ye Ice-falls! ye that from the mountain's brow
Adown enormous ravines slope amain –
Torrents, methinks, that heard a mighty voice,
And stopped at once amid their maddest plunge!
Motionless torrents! silent cataracts!
Who made you glorious as the gates of Heaven
Beneath the keen full moon? Who bade the sun
Clothe you with rainbows? Who, with living flowers
Of loveliest blue, spread garlands at your feet? –
God! let the torrents, like a shout of nations,
Answer! and let the ice-plains echo, God!
God! sing ye meadow-streams with gladsome voice!
Ye pine-groves, with your soft and soul-like sounds!
And they too have a voice, yon piles of snow,
And in their perilous fall shall thunder, God!

Ye living flowers that skirt the eternal frost!
Ye wild goats sporting round the eagle's nest!
Ye eagles, play-mates of the mountain-storm!
Ye lightnings, the dread arrows of the clouds!
Ye signs and wonders of the element!
Utter forth God, and fill the hills with praise!

Thou too, hoar Mount! with thy sky-pointing peaks,
Oft from whose feet the avalanche, unheard,
Shoots downward, glittering through the pure serene
Into the depth of clouds, that veil thy breast –
Thou too again, stupendous Mountain! thou
That as I raise my head, awhile bowed low
In adoration, upward from thy base
Slow travelling with dim eyes suffused with tears,
Solemnly seemest, like a vapoury cloud,
To rise before me – Rise, O ever rise,
Rise like a cloud of incense from the Earth!
Thou kingly Spirit throned among the hills,
Thou dread ambassador from Earth to Heaven,
Great Hierarch! tell thou the silent sky,
And tell the stars, and tell yon rising sun,
Earth, with her thousand voices, praises God.

As we approach the season of Epiphany with which this anthology will end, I want to give you a series of epiphanies or glimpses of the Divine from a variety of poets. We have had the unlooked-for and almost resisted epiphany that came to Hardy from the 'Darkling Thrush', the epiphany that Tennyson heard and felt in the New Year's wild bells, and the disclosure of the true sublime Ruth Pitter heard in the bird in the tree. Today and tomorrow we read of epiphanies that two very different poets saw in the winter snows themselves, in the frost that glittered and shone as a window for the glories that nature veils. Coleridge, best known for a small handful of poems, chiefly 'The Rime of the Ancient Mariner' and 'Kubla Khan', which come to us like floating fragments from the vast shipwreck of his life, was, in everything he wrote, profoundly aware of the divine root of all things, of heaven in ordinary, of the moments of epiphany, transcendence and transfigured vision that may strike at us at any time. Even before his return to a fully articulated Trinitarian and orthodox Christianity, he intuited that the phenomena of nature were themselves the words in a poem, a kind of divine language:

The lovely shapes and sounds intelligible
Of that eternal language, which thy God
Utters, who from eternity doth teach
Himself in all, and all things in himself.
('Frost at Midnight')

Today's psalm-like incantation, a kind of glorious mountain-top outburst to lift our January hearts, has a curious history. Though the poem is grandly titled 'Hymn Before Sunrise, in the Vale of Chamouni', Coleridge had in fact never been to Switzerland, let alone the 'Vale of Chamouni'; and in the dark and difficult days, when he was struggling with addiction and heartbreak, in which he wrote this poem, he was unlikely to have been up anywhere before sunrise. But nevertheless, the poem describes a vivid and true experience whose geography has been strangely transposed without in any way diminishing its spiritual music.

The actual experience of which this part of the poem is a true record occurred on Scafell Pike in the Lake District, when Coleridge was climbing it alone, and was recorded in a letter to Sara Hutchinson, the woman with whom he was tragically and impossibly in love. And the epiphany came at a moment of terror in which he was stuck partway down a cliff and could neither rise nor descend:

My Limbs were all in a tremble – I lay upon my Back to rest myself, & was beginning according to my Custom to laugh at myself for a Madman, when the sight of the Crags above me on each side, & the impetuous Clouds just over them, posting so luridly & so rapidly northward, overawed me. I lay in a state of almost prophetic Trance & Delight – & blessed God aloud, for the powers of Reason & the Will, which remaining no Danger can overpower us! O God, I exclaimed aloud – how calm, how blessed am I now ... (*Collected Letters*, p. 841)

Perhaps because their first expression was to a friend whose love he could not openly acknowledge, or because he felt that a grander and more famous scene would bring more clearly to his readers the sublimity he had experienced, he ended up reframing this experience in this poem. As he wrote on the day before its publication, in a letter to another friend:

> I involuntarily poured forth a Hymn in the manner of the Psalms, tho' afterwards I thought the Ideas &c disproportionate to our humble mountains – & accidentally lighting on a short Note in some swiss Poems, concerning the Vale of Chamouny, & it's Mountain, I transferred myself thither, in the Spirit, & adapted my former feelings to these grander external objects ... (*Collected Letters*, pp. 864–5)

And this poem is certainly 'a Hymn in the manner of the Psalms'. If in 'Frost at Midnight' he has seen the mountains and the clouds as God's voice speaking to us, now we hear the antiphonal return; in the voice of the poet we catch the praise of the creation back to its creator. In some ways it's a pity that Coleridge felt so ashamed of his own fraught circumstances, so unworthy of the religious epiphany he had experienced, that he felt the need to transfer it to some safe distance, for to my mind there is gospel in knowing that God gives us these experiences just where we are, on our own 'humble mountains', in the midst of our complicated, shadowed and ambiguous lives. At this moment, Coleridge the sinner was also in the fullest sense Coleridge 'the priest' of nature, a term that comes from George Herbert, as he says in his beautiful poem 'Providence', 'man is the world's high Priest'.

Of all the creatures both in sea and land
Only to Man thou hast made known thy ways,
And put the penne alone into his hand,
And made him Secretary of thy praise.

Beasts fain would sing; birds ditty to their notes;
Trees would be tuning on their native lute
To thy renown: but all their hands and throats
Are brought to Man, while they are lame and mute.

Man is the world's high Priest: he doth present
The sacrifice for all; while they below
Unto the service mutter an assent,
Such as springs use that fall, and winds that blow.

In fact, even in this transposed setting, Coleridge gently acknow-
ledges the spiritually low starting point for this moment of
revelation, even as he beautifully shows how the spirits are raised
by the sight of the mountains:

That as I raise my head, awhile bowed low
In adoration, upward from thy base
Slow travelling with dim eyes suffused with tears,
Solemnly seemest, like a vapoury cloud,
To rise before me – Rise, O ever rise

And from here on to its beautiful climax, the poem raises us all,
carries us on an ascent:

To rise before me – Rise, O ever rise
Rise like a cloud of incense from the Earth!
Thou kingly Spirit throned among the hills,
Thou dread ambassador from Earth to Heaven,
Great Hierarch! tell thou the silent sky,
And tell the stars, and tell yon rising sun,
Earth, with her thousand voices, praises God.

5 JANUARY

Rocky Mountain Railroad, Epiphany *Luci Shaw*

The steel rails parallel the river as we penetrate
ranges of pleated slopes and crests – all too complicated
for capture in a net of words. In this showing, the train window

is a lens for an alternate reality – the sky lifts and the light forms
shadows of unstudied intricacy. The multiple colors of snow
in the dimpled fresh fall. Boulders like white breasts. Edges

blunted with snow. My open-window mind is too little for
this landscape. I long for each sweep of view to toss off
a sliver, imbed it in my brain so that it will flash

and flash again its unrepeatable views. Inches. Angles.
Niches. Two eagles. A black crow. Skeletal twigs' notched
chalices for snow. Reaches of peak above peak beyond peak

Next to the track the low sun burns the silver birches into
brass candles. And always the flow of the companion river's
cord of silk links the valleys together with the probability

of continuing revelation. I mind-freeze for the future
this day's worth of disclosure. Through the glass
the epiphanies reel me in, absorbed, enlightened.

Today's Epiphany poem by Luci Shaw makes an interesting con-
trast and parallel with Coleridge's psalm-like outpouring. Both
poems are a response to the beauty of nature, and specifically to

the sight of snowy mountains, and the play of light on snow and ice. In both poems we have a sense of glory and of the sublime rising 'reaches of peak above peak beyond peak'. But the differences in tone, feel and technique are also telling. Coleridge's poem is set in an ecstatic, exultant, explicit and almost overactive key:

> let the torrents, like a shout of nations,
> Answer!

And the poetry pours out of him and into us like a torrent. Coleridge's poem is like a rephrasing of the *Benedicite* sung by a full chorus, 'Earth, with her thousand voices', praising God. It is fully participative and holds nothing in reserve. By contrast, there is something intimate, contingent and understated in Luci Shaw's poem, even though the epiphanies it offers are in their own way just as sublime and ecstatic. We know that the genesis of Coleridge's poem came when he was out on Scafell Pike, utterly immersed in the elements, and in peril of his life. This is all very well for the young, fit and adventurous, but Luci Shaw offers an equally profound and spiritual reflection on an experience that many more people are likely and able to share: the sights we see journeying into the mountains in a railway carriage. The train's rapidity, the small and constantly shifting frame of the window, the brief glimpses, no sooner seen than lost, the unrepeatable views: these restrictions and contingencies are embraced. They are not apologized for as shortcomings, but in their very brevity and incompleteness are part of the spiritual experience. It is not simply that on this occasion we see from a train window, but that as finite beings we only have 'window-minds', through which we must learn to see with a proper humility, always knowing that what we pass through, and what passes through us, is a partial and incomplete glimpse of something greater than ourselves. Reality is

> all too complicated
> for capture in a net of words.

It's worth looking in closer detail at some of the effects Luci Shaw achieves in this well-crafted poem. There are six unrhymed tercets, but, as with the technique of Robert Hayden, the apparently 'blank verse' is in fact beautifully wrought and rich with the musical effects of assonance and alliteration. This poem is quite literally poetry in motion; the series of plosives in 'parallels ... penetrate ... pleated', alternating with the 'o' sounds of 'slopes' and 'showing', pick us up and set us moving along. Shaw delicately alludes to the meanings of epiphany as both 'a showing' and a shining out:

In this showing, the train window

is a lens for an alternate reality – the sky lifts and the light forms shadows of unstudied intricacy.

Then come a series of particular individual images flashing past the window: 'Boulders like white breasts', 'Two eagles. A black crow', 'Skeletal twigs', 'Reaches of peak', 'silver birches', and constantly glimpsed, winding in and out of the different views, 'the companion river's cord of silk'. Taken by itself as a notebook jotting from a train window this would be all very good but unremarkable. The real depth and meaning of this poem emerges in Shaw's subtle metaphors, which underpin and ultimately transform what she sees until epiphany has become sacrament. The 'skeletal twigs', whose notches for a moment seem to cup the snow, are 'chalices'. Next, the 'silver birches' are transfigured into 'brass candles'. Even as she makes this play from silver to brass, the poet, like an acolyte, is laying out the altar for the poem's own sacrament: the candles at the corners, the chalice raised. And then, the landscape itself seems to have become hieratic, become the poem's priest; the companion river is a cord of silk around the mountain's snowy alb. None of this is made explicit, but works almost subliminally, in the gentle suggestion of metaphor.

The other theme, in addition to sacrament, that runs through this poem is time itself. Indeed, the two themes are related, and related precisely by the common subject of epiphany. An epiphany is a showing, given only for a distinct moment, yet of something eternal. The question always arises, how do we deal with such epiphanies? Eliot goes to the heart of the matter in the *Four Quartets*:

Quick now, here, now, always –
Ridiculous the waste sad time
Stretching before and after.
('Burnt Norton')

We no sooner have these moments of epiphany than they seem to be taken from us. The question is how we can live from them, draw from them, return to them. One answer to that question is sacrament, as a ritual return to a source of revelation, an anamnesis in which the past becomes present again. One might perhaps think of the sacraments, each time they are celebrated, as a series of glimpses, from a window of a moving train, onto the same divine landscape, sustaining the voyager, and giving a gift of hope: what Shaw in this poem calls 'the probability of continuing revelation'.

There is a final and beautiful turn at the end of this poem. It is customary to speak of the flashing and moving images that go past a train or car window as something that we 'reel in', or pictures that are reeled into us. But this is Epiphany, and what we see in Epiphany is always greater than what we are. Luci Shaw's last line reverses the flow. We do not reel in the epiphanies; they pull us out into themselves. There is perhaps some long reach between the image of the net at the opening of the poem and that of the reel at its close. It begins with a confession that we cannot do the catching – our 'net of words' will never be adequate for the reality that slips through them – but it ends with a confession that we ourselves are caught, and glad to be caught, to be reeled in to a reality beyond us. Indeed, in this final image, she may be gently alluding to the gospel idea of fishing for people (Matthew 4.19):

Through the glass
the epiphanies reel me in, absorbed, enlightened.

6 JANUARY

The Divine Image *William Blake*

To Mercy, Pity, Peace, and Love
All pray in their distress;
And to these virtues of delight
Return their thankfulness.

For Mercy, Pity, Peace, and Love
Is God, our father dear,
And Mercy, Pity, Peace, and Love
Is Man, his child and care.

For Mercy has a human heart,
Pity a human face,
And Love, the human form divine,
And Peace, the human dress.

Then every man, of every clime,
That prays in his distress,
Prays to the human form divine,
Love, Mercy, Pity, Peace.

And all must love the human form,
In heathen, Turk, or Jew;
Where Mercy, Love, and Pity dwell
There God is dwelling too.

The Feast of the Epiphany celebrates the visit of the magi to the Christ-child, and so the inclusion of the Gentiles in the gospel story: and not simply the Gentiles in a generic way, but all the distinct races, cultures and religions of 'the nations'; this is one reason why the tradition of depicting the three wise men as representing three different races is so helpful. On this feast day, it might seem obvious to choose one of the well-known poems that recall or describe that familiar scene: Eliot's 'The Journey of the Magi', or Yeats' poem 'The Magi'. Already in this anthology a number of poems have described the events of the Epiphany. Cairns gave us a glimpse of the kings on their way:

Across the ridge,
three wise men spur three horses

towards a star.

And Belloc gave us that ambiguous image of 'the kings at arms' worshipping the Christ-child, perhaps by taking him into their arms, perhaps by laying their arms at his feet.

But I wanted in this final poem to move from the outward and visible picture that adorns so many of the Christmas cards we will be taking down today, and as those outward images fade away, to come through poetry to the inward and spiritual truth which they proclaim. And that spiritual truth is that in the Incarnation Christ, in assuming human nature, takes on, becomes involved in, visits and redeems the whole of humanity, not just the chosen people to whose race and culture he belonged. And what is more, when the fullness of God comes to dwell in the fullness of Christ's humanity, then that mysterious 'image of God' in which all humanity was made (Genesis 1.27) is at last restored, and we can see the Light who so uniquely and particularly became the Christ-child at Bethlehem. As John's Gospel clearly proclaims, 'The true light, which enlightens everyone, was coming into the world' (John 1.9). It seems to me that William Blake's poem 'The Divine Image', rather than any specifically Christmas or Epiphany verse, goes to the heart of these things.

'The Divine Image' first appeared as 'Song 18' in *Songs of Innocence* in 1789, and then again in the remarkable *Songs of*

Innocence and of Experience, when Blake came to engrave and print those together in 1794. In some ways the key line of this whole poem is the second one: 'All pray in their distress'. Blake does not begin with the clearly different dogmas and teachings, proclamations and conclusions, of various faiths, but starts instead at their common experiences of supplication and need. And this is an approach that has great integrity. We may wish, in our liberal and even-handed way, to come to a conclusion that since there is one God, all religions must 'be the same', but this would be equally insulting to all religions. We should listen to our neighbours who do not share our faith, and do them the courtesy of taking our differences seriously, as they should do for us. But acknowledging those differences does not mean alienating ourselves from them or denying their humanity. On the contrary, we recognize one another's needs in the very act of sharing notes on our faith. Rather surprisingly, Rudyard Kipling put this extremely well in a brief verse that may be drawing on this Blake poem, in *Plain Tales from the Hills*:

My brother kneels, so saith Kabir,
To stone and brass in heathen-wise,
But in my brother's voice I hear
My own unanswered agonies.
His God is as his fates assign
His prayer is all the world's – and mine.

Though Blake starts with this common experience of prayer, he does in fact draw his beautiful, universal gospel ('The Everlasting Gospel', as he called it) from a distinctively Judaeo-Christian idea, which is the notion that we are made in God's image. Therefore human compassion – 'Mercy, Pity, Peace, and Love' – must have a divine origin wherever it is encountered, in whatever religion. Of course, it could be countered that we do not always find mercy, pity, peace and love in others' humanity or even in our own, but this is where the antithetical structure of the *Songs of Innocence and of Experience* helps to bring a depth and balance. In this poem, Blake writes:

For Mercy has a human heart,
Pity a human face,
And Love, the human form divine,
And Peace, the human dress.

He also wrote a shorter poem, which first appeared in the earlier *Songs of Experience*, titled significantly '*A* Divine Image' – not '*The* Divine Image'. In this poem he replies to the above with some bitter words:

Cruelty has a human heart,
And Jealousy a human face;
Terror the human form divine,
And secrecy the human dress.

The human dress is forged iron,
The human form a fiery forge,
The human face a furnace seal'd,
The human heart its hungry gorge.

And as we read this searing and compelling verse we must confess that this is also true. But there is a real distinction in the way the two poems are framed. In the *earlier* version there is no equivalent to this second verse of 'The Divine Image':

For Mercy, Pity, Peace, and Love
Is God, our father dear,
And Mercy, Pity, Peace, and Love
Is Man, his child and care.

So although the cruelty, jealousy, terror and secrecy are ascribed to humanity, in that poem they are never ascribed to God. Likewise, there is an extraordinary paradox in which even in our utterly fallen and darkened humanity, dressed in secrecy with our faces sealed rather than open and our hearts hungry rather than giving, Blake cannot forbear to follow the term 'the human form' with the word Divine. Somewhere beneath these 'forgeries' (and

Blake is clearly playing on the word 'forge') and deceptions, there is still the divine image in us, waiting to be restored. It is that restoration that begins at Christmas and shines out at Epiphany.

Today's poem has a final turn, which is telling and prophetic in the deepest sense of that word – prophecy as unveiling truth and also speaking to our times, speaking truth to power – and that turn is the movement from prayer to love. The penultimate verse notes how we pray in our distress to 'the human form divine', with its upward motion taking our humanity to the 'form divine' in heaven in prayer. The final verse brings us back down to earth and shows us that the consequence of recognizing 'the human form divine' in our prayers is that we must recognize and love it in our neighbours. It is well known that Blake lived in almost complete obscurity and was not famous in his own day. But among those very few people who visited him, who held in their hands a copy of *The Songs of Innocence and of Experience* and recognized a little of his prophetic genius, was Samuel Taylor Coleridge. Introduced to Blake by a mutual friend, a Swedenborgian, August Tulk, Coleridge was lent a precious copy of *The Songs of Innocence and of Experience* signed by Blake himself. Tulk, together with Coleridge, was working to see how the insights in *The Songs* could be used directly to motivate people in the amelioration of conditions for children employed in factories. And indeed Coleridge himself, in a poem written some time before he met Blake but not long after Blake had written this poem, expressed most deeply and perfectly that link between prayer and love with which I wish to end this anthology; so that prayers which may have been deepened for us by the poetry in this book may bear fruit in love. Coleridge wrote, in 'The Rime of the Ancient Mariner', words that capture the heart of the Blake poem:

He prayeth best, who loveth best
All things both great and small;
For the dear God who loveth us,
He made and loveth all.

But we will leave the last word to Blake himself:

And all must love the human form,
In heathen, Turk, or Jew;
Where Mercy, Love, and Pity dwell
There God is dwelling too.

References

Chesterton, G. K., *Orthodoxy: The Original Classic Edition*, Emereo Publishing, 2012.

Coleridge, S. T., *Biographia Literaria*, edited by James Engell and W. Jackson Bate, Princeton, 1983.

Coleridge, S. T., *Collected Letters of Samuel Taylor Coleridge*, edited by Earl Leslie Griggs, 6 vols, Oxford University Press, 1956–71, vol. 2.

Dante Alighieri, *The Divine Comedy*, I 'Inferno', translated by Robin Kirkpatrick, Penguin Classics, 2006.

Dante Alighieri, *The New Life (La Vita Nuova)*, translated by Dante Gabriel Rossetti, London: Ellis and Elvey, 1899. Accessible Project Gutenberg, https://archive.org/details/new lifelavitanuooodantrich.

Eliot, T. S., *Choruses from The Rock*, Faber, 1934.

Eliot, T. S., *Four Quartets*, Faber, 1943.

Guite, Malcolm, *Faith, Hope and Poetry*, Ashgate, 2010.

Guite, Malcolm, *Sounding the Seasons*, Canterbury Press, 2012.

Guite, Malcolm, *The Word in the Wilderness*, Canterbury Press, 2014.

Larkin, Philip, 'Afternoons', in *The Whitsun Weddings*, Faber, 1964.

Lewis, C. S., *A Preface to Paradise Lost*, Oxford University Press, 1942, reprinted 1969.

Acknowledgement of Sources

Dave Baird, 'Autumn', first appeared in *Christendom Review* www.christendomreview.com/Volume006Issue001/poetry_ 014.html, used by permission of the author.

Richard Bauckham, 'Song of the Shepherds', used by permission of the author.

Scott Cairns, 'Annunciation' and 'Nativity', in *Idiot Psalms*, Paraclete Press, 2014, used by permission of the author.

Malcolm Guite, 'Launde Abbey on St Lucy's Day', to appear in *Parable and Paradox*, Canterbury Press, forthcoming 2016.

Malcolm Guite, 'O Antiphon Sonnets' and 'Refugee', in *Sounding the Seasons*, Canterbury Press, 2012.

David Grieve, 'Advent Good Wishes', used by permission of the author.

Robert Hayden, 'Those Winter Sundays', from *Collected Poems*, Liveright Publishing Corporation, 1966, used with permission.

Grevel Lindop, 'The Moons' and 'For Our Lady of Guadalupe', in *Luna Park*, Carcanet Press, 2015, used by permission of the author.

Ruth Pitter, 'The Bird in the Tree', in *The Spirit Watchers*, Cresset Press, 1939, used with permission.

Anne Ridler, 'Christmas and Common Birth', in *The Nine Bright Shiners*, Faber, 1943, used with permission.

Luci Shaw, 'Kenosis', in *Harvesting Fog*, Pinion Publishing, 2010, and 'Rocky Mountain Railroad, Epiphany', used by permission of the author.

Printed in the USA
CPSIA information can be obtained
at www.ICGtesting.com
JSHW081002291123
52945JS00002B/23